flush all those bad tapes
the shrink man said
get all of those negative thoughts
out of your head

the ain't fair blues recording
is wearing mighty thin
think positively about yourself
that's how to begin

i know it will take some time
we all walk before we fly
be honest and trust
   those old gut feelings
say yes to your life and try

Kim

The Art of Hanging Loose in an Uptight World

Featuring Psychological Exercises for Personal Growth

Dr. Ken Olson

FAWCETT CREST • NEW YORK

THE ART OF HANGING LOOSE IN AN UPTIGHT WORLD

Published by Fawcett Crest Books, a unit of CBS Publications, the Consumer Publishing Division of CBS Inc., by arrangement with O'Sullivan, Woodside and Company.

ISBN: 0-449-23613-7

Printed in the United States of America

16 15 14 13 12 11 10 9 8 7

This book is dedicated to my wife,
Jeannie,
who always stood by me;
and to our three children,
Mike, Danny and Jan,
who have brought us,
as parents,
such great joy.

The Art of
Hanging Loose
in an Uptight
World

Contents

Chapter III

"It Ain't Fair Blues"

Chapter IV

The Perfectionist

Chapter V

How to Turn Off the Negative Tapes and Hang Loose

Chapter VI

Marriage—the First Fifty Years Are the Hardest

Chapter VII

These People We Call
Our Sons and Daughters   137

Chapter VIII

Strictly Personal   183

Psychological Exercises   195

The Art of
Hanging Loose
in an Uptight
World

Introduction

Olson, Kenneth: of course, that is the way names are listed. Those initials O.K. tell it like it is. Dr. O.K. is OK!

Believing people can find hope through changing and improving, plus peace in living a life of love, while loving the life they live, he guides, with his inherent sagacity, and teaches people—as people, not as patients.

Dr. O.K. is a people person. He listens and observes; then offers options and alternatives. When he feels people are clinging to negative tapes recorded in their heart, he helps them seek and flip the 'off' switch, while gently but firmly reinforcing positive potentials.

The Art Of Hanging Loose

For those he touches, his candle provides an environment for enlightened decisions, demystifies the weighing and sorting of values, and facilitates facing personal responsibilities.

Without help, problems and grief may result in destructive life styles. With his help, there is an opportunity to work through problems and grief in a creative manner. In a crisis he is flexible, yet all the while forever stable.

In our world many acquire knowledge in multiple fields. Wisdom, however, is revealed through understanding that knowledge and recognizing its relevance. Dr. O.K. handles that easily. He consociates his knowledge and experience, wisdom and talents, then shares all with people. From there it can be flight or fight that he has fortified with right.

'Hanging Loose' as we go is truly an art of the highest form. In the practice of this art, no one parallels this author.

Dr. O.K. is the master of this art.

From one of the many people he has touched.

1

It's an Uptight World

One does not have to be a social scientist or psychologist or a great seer of the future to know that we live in uptight times. When I was a child, one of the radio programs that I was most afraid of was *Lights Out*. Today the program that strikes more fear in the hearts of the American people is the six o'clock news.

We don't live in a time of future shock, but of daily shock; hourly shock. If we think yesterday's news was bad, we fear that tomorrow's will be worse, so we dare not cheer up at all. There are feelings among us of huddling around the TV in the candle glow, courageously turning on the news to see what other scandal, what other shockwave, what other war or disaster or murder has hit our world. We live in an uptight time.

The world in which we live has been reduced in size so that what happens in one section of the world affects us all. In fact, we feel as if the whole world is crowded into a telephone booth. The realities of our time speak for themselves. Wars, riots, families breaking down, the drug culture, the energy crisis have frightened so many people that they are perplexed, anxious and helpless as to what is coming next and wondering if there is anything a person can do to calm the desperation. The increase in the consumption of alcohol is an alarming symptom of a troubled people.

The purpose of this book is not to make light of our times or to make it a Pollyanna world; but the first premise is that we do live in an uptight world. Change, crisis, chaos, stress. They are facts. The next thing we need to ask ourselves is how to live in this kind of a world. Thus the purpose of the book is to try, in a small way, to teach people the art of hanging loose.

Two dominant emotions seem to prevail in our country, and probably in our world itself; and they are depression and fear. Have you ever observed people as they walk across a street? How many of them are walking with their heads bowed; the burdens of their life too heavy? Or have you seen the tension and the frustration on the face of the driver in another automobile as he struggles to fight his way through the traffic to his home, through smog, and hopes he has enough gas to make it. We do need in this time to learn how to hang loose.

I discovered the secret of the art of hanging loose many years ago quite by accident. And like so many things we do right, we often do not remember how right they are, or how important they are to keep repeating them. But I did some right things to hang loose, and many years later I discovered the powerful significance of how to hang loose.

In 1951 Jeannie, my new bride, and I arrived in Minneapolis to enter Northwestern Lutheran Theological Seminary. She worked as a legal secretary and I soon became restless about not being a provider as a man. Someone told me you could sell Watkins Products door-to-door and make good money. I didn't know what Watkins Products were, but he said you might possibly make $2.00 an hour, and in 1951 that seemed like a lot of money.

I went to the distributor, got my kit of vanilla, cinnamon, spices, Christmas cards, linament, cologne, perfume and coconut oil shampoo. He said, "Here's our territory. Start ringing doorbells."

I like people so I was glad to ring their doorbells and say, "Hi, I'm your friendly Watkins man! Would you like a free sample of vanilla?"

But once in a while, I would encounter that woman who would treat my very act of ringing the doorbell as a catastrophe, an invasion of her privacy. She would attack me as an interloper; would yell and curse at me.

I would say, "Lady, I'm just trying to sell some

The Art Of Hanging Loose

Watkins Products. I'm sorry if I disturbed you. Thank you for your time." The door was slammed.

Now, the important thing that I did at that moment in time was also the most important thing of all! In the seminary preparing for the ministry they *did* stress becoming acquainted with the Bible. I recalled that passage where Jesus gave instruction to the seventy to go out two-by-two, door-to-door. He said that when you come to a house that doesn't receive you well, shake the dust off your feet before you leave for the next one. Now I remembered. Shake the bad memory of that rejection. Shake it from you! Shake it off your feet, and leave it at that doorstep before you ring that next bell. And also, in seminary you were taught to pray for people, so as I walked down the sidewalk I offered a prayer for the husband that lived with that bitch. I had her for thirty seconds, but he'll have her waiting for him every night.

So I laughed and chuckled to myself. Little did I know that what I had just done at that moment in time was to be able to stop a rejection tape, or series of negative thoughts; thoughts that, if I allowed them to continue, would have made me very depressed, discouraged, and defeated. But I was hanging loose. I just couldn't wait to ring the next doorbell. And I kept finding wonderful people who were nice to me. When it was twenty degrees below zero some would invite me in for coffee and cookies, and as an added bonus, would give me an order to make me feel even better.

In An Uptight World

I was so enthusiastic about the money that could be made by selling Watkins I encouraged nine other married seminarians with children to become salesmen. I told them of the money that could be made, about being your own boss, working at your own pace, and of my success. They all signed up, they were trained and they all quit, one after the other. I didn't know why, and I don't think they did either. They said my area was better than theirs. I knew that was not true.

Years later I began to realize that what they did was play a rejection tape. They began to think about how that woman had treated them, how she had been mean to them and how it wasn't fair. Here they were, just poor students, working their way through seminary, trying to be good men of the cloth, with wives and children to support. They thought about how some woman had screamed and bellowed at them when they hadn't done anything to hurt her. Off they would go looking at their next door and the next long sidewalk, and they probably muttered to themselves, "I hope no one is home here." A few more calls, a few more rejections and they would turn around and go home.

Winter in Minneapolis is never an exciting time, so the next day they could say it looked awfully cold out there. Besides, the people weren't very nice yesterday, and they probably wouldn't sell anything today either. Because they didn't ring doorbells, they didn't sell.

I had a secret—a secret to keep me hanging loose

emotionally and not getting uptight over rejection. The secret of learning how to break up a negative, destructive and disturbing thought pattern is so powerful that it means an individual has a great deal of influence over how he is going to feel and react emotionally.

A negative tape, as I use the concept, refers to an habitual thought pattern in which, once the "on button" is pushed, the negative thoughts soon evoke negative emotions which recall a series of similar bad memories from the past that go on and on and on until they hypnotize you and claim power over your mind. If you've done any reading on the power of positive thinking you know what a miraculous thing repetition can be. It convinces the subconscious and the subconscious tells the conscious. Pretty soon your whole body is buying whatever it is the subconscious is selling.

The one major drawback is that the subconscious is neither good nor bad and it doesn't recognize the difference. It's full of power however, and you have to be very careful what it is you're directing it to learn.

In a way it's like the outlet on your wall. It's full of electricity and it has no way of distinguishing right from wrong. Therefore, if you stick your finger in the outlet it is going to turn the full force of its power on your finger—but if you plug in your radio, you'll get music for your effort. The electricity is neither good nor bad. The power is there, waiting to be used. *How* you use it is your decision to make; and that's the way it is with your subconscious mind. Feed it negative thoughts and it will give you negative results. Feed it positive thoughts and it will give you positive results. The power is there. How you use it is your decision to make.

It is possible to break negative or destructive thought patterns. You can control your emotional reactions. After all, emotions are ours, not the other way around.

How often are you in charge of what is happening to you? Are you guilty of waiting for someone's action to dictate your frame of mind? Is your life pattern that of waiting for someone else to make you feel good or important? And then, if no one causes an action which in turn make you REact, do you feel that you've been ignored or that no one cares? In short, do you feel convinced that others are responsible for the way you feel?

I've got a bulletin: nobody makes you feel any way you don't want to feel.

So somebody was curt. That's *his* problem. Whatever happened that made him hostile happened to him, not you. He has to live with it. You don't. Of course, if you're looking for sympathy and an excuse for a drink or a good cry, well, there you are. Old so and so was curt to you. Bottoms up.

The truth of the matter is that you more than anyone else in your world determine the state of your emotions. If someone offends or hurts or disappoints you it's because you have given him the power to do so. When you realize that, you will become master of your emotions. Until then you're a human yo-yo being bounced up and down and around by the changing attitudes of others.

No, this isn't another book on positive thinking. If you have a negative tape going and you try to become positive in your thinking before you learn how to destroy it you will only become positively negative.

It helps to have a realistic view of the world in which you live and the people with whom you live. In wanting them to be different and wishing for them to change, you become the proverbial ostrich hiding your head in the sand (and you know what shows when you do that). The only person you have power to change is you, and you can begin by destroying or turning off your negative thoughts.

Remember what you chanted as a kid when someone yelled "chicken" or "four-eyes" or "bird legs" at you? "Sticks and stones may break my bones, but words can never hurt me." That's a myth, of course. Sticks and stones can break our bones but words can break our hearts, and the hearts of those around us. Words of condemnation, words of accusation, words of self-doubt are negative. They are mind-breakers and will-benders. They chase away friends and turn us into lonely, nasty tempered souls. I like better the old proverb which goes "Ten men cannot do the destruction to me that I can do to myself." That, friend, is TRUTH.

In An Uptight World

For a number of years now I have had the pleasure of learning to love a lot of different kinds of kids. Some have problems with parents, some come from broken homes, others are welfare cases, and a good many of them have been involved in the drug scene. I will never forget the reply to my question to Suzy, an 18-year-old drug addict, who had just been released from a reform school, "What did you learn during those nine months?" One of the things she said she learned during her stay was the truth of the slogan, "You are your own bummer!" She even kept a handwritten reminder of the message over her vanity mirror. She told me, "I used to blame my parents, the school, the establishment, anybody and everybody, except myself for my shooting dope and later for my getting locked up. As long as I could blame others for my behavior I didn't have to face the fact that no one bummed me out but me. I did it with my own thinking."

This girl had discovered a real truth—that the enemy is within—that no one can bum us out or make us feel as badly as the way we ourselves can when we dwell on negative experiences. These are the bummers I call negative tapes.

2

"What if . . . ?"

The *What If . . . ?* tape is based on fear and worry. It has a peculiar appetite. It feeds on more fear and worry. *What If . . . ?* is afraid to make a mistake. It says, *"What If* this goes wrong?" *"What If* that goes wrong?"

One Friday morning after a session of group therapy, an extremely shy eighteen-year-old we'll call Ann came up timidly and said, "Dr. Olson, could you help me?" She had been in our group all week. We had just come from an hour-and-a-half session, and suddenly she was speaking up, asking for help.

I said to her. "Well, we've got ten minutes before

I have to go to the outpatient clinic. What can I do for you?"

"I'm going home this weekend," she replied softly, and I said, "Is that bad?" She shook her head. "No," she said. "That's good."

"Then what's the problem?"

"Well," she paused, looked at her shoes then back up at me. "I'm going out Saturday night with my boyfriend."

I waited. There had to be more. There was no more, so I said, "Is that the problem?"

She blushed.

I said, "You don't *have* to go out with him."

"Oh no," she said quickly. "I like him. I really do."

"Then I don't understand."

"It's—well, we're going out to dinner and—everytime I eat with a boy—I vomit."

I shook my head and sighed in relief. "Oh, Annie," I said, "I was afraid it was something serious."

She looked at me in surprise. "It's very serious."

"All right. If you're serious about asking me for help, you'll have to do exactly as I say."

She agreed.

"You must follow the instructions precisely," I said, and she bobbed her head.

"I will. What are they?"

"First of all you must admit it."

"Admit what?"

"That you're a vomiter. That you vomit easily."

She was dumbfounded and then she began to laugh, actually giggle.

I went on sternly, "You said you wanted help. Now I have four minutes left and this is what you're going to do. It's ten-thirty on Friday morning and already you're beginning to think 'What If I vomit tomorrow night.' 'What If I can't make it to the ladies' room in time.' Am I right?"

"Right," she whispered.

"You're thinking 'What If I throw up in his car? Wouldn't that be terrible? What would he think of me?' Worse yet, 'What If I throw up on the table?' Aren't you thinking those things?"

She said, "Yes, all of it."

"In fact," I went on, "you're probably manufacturing butterflies in your stomach this very minute, just visualizing tomorrow night—and here this is only Friday morning. Now, you're going to be in great shape for your date if you keep playing that *What If . . . ?* tape." I paused for effect, then continued, "Here's the plan. I want you to say to yourself when you wake up tomorrow morning, 'I, Annie, am a vomiter. I am the world's greatest vomiter.' Then I want you to picture yourself going into a very elegant restaurant and, as you walk in, I want you to see yourself looking at the *maitre d'* and smiling. 'Guess who's here?' you're telling yourself. 'Annie the vomiter! The world's champion thrower-upper has come to your nice restaurant.' As you walk on by I want you to look at the waiters and think these thoughts, 'Get your buckets and your mops, fellows, 'cause Annie the vomiter is here tonight.' "

Annie's horror turned, again, to giggles. "I couldn't," she protested.

So I told her, "You have to. You have to sit down tomorrow night in that restaurant and look at the tablecloth and then at your boyfriend and think about how funny he's going to look when the world's greatest vomiter does her thing. Concentrate on it, Ann. Don't let your mind wander."

She thought for a moment, then she nodded. "Yes, I'll do it," she said. "I'll try."

Monday morning she came back to the clinic and I asked her how it went. "Well," she sighed, "I started out Saturday morning thinking *What If . . . ?* I even told myself that you were crazy. But if I thought *What If* I vomit all day I'd never be able to go out that night. I was so desperate that I had to try it your way. So I started to say, 'I, Annie, am the world's greatest vomiter' over and over to myself. Then I started laughing. It *was* silly. I felt stupid.

"That night my boyfriend picked me up, and when we were seated at the restaurant he said, 'You've been mumbling all evening. What's going on?' So I told him."

"What did you say?"

"I told him the whole thing. I told him what I was afraid of, that of vomiting tonight, and what you told me to say to myself all day long and what to say to myself as we entered the restaurant. He just roared with laughter. So did I," she said, "and people looked at us like we were insane which made everything even funnier. I never enjoyed a meal so much in my whole life."

The *What If . . . ?* tape is foreboding—until it's ridiculed. Fear is a stern taskmaster, even though most of the things we fear or worry over never happen. Still we continue to pay the price emotionally by allowing ourselves to get uptight. The *hypothetical What If . . . ?* IS capable of giving us very real headaches, heart attacks and ulcers. Only the result of worry is real—not the worry itself. The *What If . . . ?* tape is granted power by people who allow it to have authority. They play it over and over until they believe it. Then they become so brittle and so frightened and so accident prone that sometimes they actually exercise their own self-fulfilling prophecy.

Some years ago a girl of thirteen was brought to me because she had been expelled from school after fainting thirty times in two months. She was such a poor insurance risk the school, fearful of being sued as the result of an accidental injury, could no longer afford to have her fainting on school property.

The parents, who had accompanied the girl, brought with them a list of the days, hours, and places where she had fainted. They also had a medical report which said there was no physiological or neurological reason why this girl should be fainting.

That left me with little to conclude except that the child was deeply involved with a *What If . . . ?* tape. Those around her helped fulfill her *What If . . . ?* prophecy. For instance, every time she would reach forward to pick up a pencil her teacher would jump up to catch her, thinking the girl was about to fall in a faint.

I looked over the charts and the calendars and the record of her daily fainting, and I put the papers on the desk behind me and said to the girl, "I guess I should be impressed, but I'm not. If I'm here to cure you of fainting you're going to have to faint. Now, show me what kind of a fainter you are. You may fall on the couch if you like, or you can lie there and faint. Or you can sit in a chair and faint if that would be more comfortable for you."

She stared at me, her face getting redder by the second. Then she said with more than a little agitation, "I can't faint just like that. What are you asking me to do? I can't faint by command."

I shrugged my shoulders. "Well," I said, "how can I cure you if you won't faint? I don't know whether you faint to the front or to the back or to the sides—or which side you go to first. I'd like to know what kind of a fainter I'm dealing with if I'm going to cure you."

She was so angry she couldn't speak for a full minute.

"Go ahead," I told her, "show me." And she swallowed and said, "I just can't faint." So I said,

"Well, then explain how I am supposed to stop you from fainting if you won't faint?" And the madder she got, the more I insisted she demonstrate her remarkable fainting ability. Needless to say she left my office without having fainted.

When she came back for her next appointment I said to her, "When I asked you to faint, you were so shocked and angry with me I'm sure you thought your parents had brought you to the craziest shrink in town. Am I right?"

She nodded. "I told all of my friends that I went to a shrink for help and that he needs the help." Then she added, "I told them what you asked me to do."

"You're still mad at me, aren't you?"

She gave me a direct answer packed with thirteen year old candor. "How could you ask me to do something that stupid?" For the next few minutes I listened to this child tell me I was nuts, insensitive, et cetera. She worked herself up into such a state of agitation and refused so adamantly to faint that she never did again.

My little thirteen year old was cured of fainting but there was no magic involved. I had, however, placed her in an interesting predicament. I reasoned that if fear was going to control our relationship I accepted the obvious. I accepted her message: *I am a fainter.* I said, "Okay, you're a fainter. Show me."

She had been placed in a paradoxical situation. At one level I told her to go ahead and faint. If she fainted she would be simply following my instructions. If she did *not* faint, then she would be following the second level instruction which was the contract, therapeutically speaking, to *cure me of my fainting behavior.* What I'm saying is that if she fainted or if she didn't faint—no matter which way she moved—she would be following my command. This is what psychotherapists call a therapeutic double-bind.

Incidentally, much later, the girl and I became friends but I never did find the reason for her fainting. We talked about her shyness and some of her other fears, and at the end of the first months of therapy I discharged her. However, ironically enough, the principal of the elementary school she attended would not let her participate in the graduation ceremonies because *he* was afraid she might faint! He had his own *What If . . . ?* tape going.

The happy ending to this story is that after several months I received an invitation to attend her graduation from charm school, her way of saying, 'Hey "Doc", look at me. Out here in front of all of these people and I'm not even worried about *What If* I faint.'

I've said that fear is a stern taskmaster, and it is. It can immobilize, rule, and ruin a person's life if it gets the upper hand. Look at what it did to Bill, a fourteen year old boy who had gone through a number of traumatic events in his short life—a broken home and problems with siblings among them. His entire world, built on a shaky foundation initially, was now crumbling around him, and out of such trauma came a fear so intense he couldn't function enough to leave his home to attend school.

At our initial meeting he told me the nature of his fear, or the form which it took, and I have to admit it was a new one on me. Bill said that during the day, although not every day but often enough, he would feel a mass of hard air bump him on the shoulder, and he knew it was his warning that something horrible was going to happen to him that night.

"What would that be?" I wanted to know. He told me that after he went to bed, when the lights were out and the room was dark, he would have the feeling of a Presence. The hard mass of air, about the size of a fist, would make him count to a hundred compulsively. With each progressive number he said the knot of air would grow larger and larger until, finally, at one hundred it would encompass the entire room. It would crush against him causing him to gasp for air and would squeeze so hard he thought he would explode. Finally he would scream in terror and only then would it disappear.

I mulled this over for a few minutes. It was, indeed, a peculiar knot of air. It thumped him on the shoulder, it grew, it had Presence, it squeezed him. Anything that smart, I told Bill, ought to have a name. And, of course, anyone knows that the person who bestows the name is the master. After all, pets don't name their owners and babies don't name parents. We tossed around one name after another for awhile before we decided it would be nice to have a name with a little fun to it, something we could laugh at. Hence the name Mr. Blob. Once it was determined that if he felt this Presence at his shoulder during the day he would say something to the effect of, "Look, Mr. Blob, I'm busy now but I'll see you tonight in my room." Sure enough, a few days later Bill encountered Mr. Blob again and he acknowledged the Presence and agreed to see him that night. However, once the lights were out it was Bill who made the first advance.

According to his account he said, "Come on now, Mr. Blob. I'm inviting you in—on my terms." And, on cue, here came the knot of air about the size of a fist and Bill began his compulsive counting. But, according to my instructions, he counted backwards. And between counts Bill said, "Mr. Blob, I'm going to destroy you. I'm going to continue to count down from one hundred and with each number you will grow smaller and smaller. And if you return after tonight I'll again reduce you to nothingness by counting down." The result was that Mr. Blob eventually disappeared, which is not to say that Bill was miraculously free of all his problems, but the overriding tyranny of that particular fear was exposed and dispelled. The idea is that once we accept fear, once we ridicule it and laugh at it, we can then deal with it out in the open. It simply cannot stand the power of laughter.

In An Uptight World

If I thought Bill's problem was the most unique, it was because at that time I had not yet encountered Terry. As he explained when he first came to my office for help, "Doc, when I turn the page of a book I can't let go. I keep turning it and turning it and turning it and, finally, if I can pretend that I'm somebody else I can let go of the paper." He went on to describe how fear had ruled his life. His mother had told him that she had a fear similar to his when she was a girl. She felt that if she left home, even briefly, something terrible would happen to her house and to her parents.

As he explained his mother's fear to me I realized the young man had been conditioned to fear since early childhood. In fact, whether she realized it or not, what the mother had actually done was transfer her fear to her son. He admitted to me that he had always felt the burden of responsibility for his family was on his shoulders. Catch the word *always*. He had felt that way since he was little more than a toddler. Now a child does not understand how he can have such magical powers that he alone can ward off floods and burglars and earthquakes, but since the responsibility was his, and since indeed these things had never happened to their home, then it must be because of his presence. The longer they went without being burglarized or flooded or otherwise hit by disaster, the more convinced he was that he must never leave his doorstep. His version of his mother's inherited tape was, 'What If I left home?

It would go up in smoke! What If it fell into a crack in the earth while I was away? It would be my fault.'

Terry was so completely tyrannized that when he would leave the family room in the evening after watching television and attempt to go through the kitchen, past the living room, down the hall, and into his bedroom, it was sheer agony. This is what would happen.

As Terry would approach the entrance to the kitchen he would begin to rock back and forth trying to drum up the courage to go through the doorway. But he couldn't. He would stand there swaying and wanting to go through but unable to do so. Finally he would convince himself that he was someone else. His reasoning was simple enough to follow. He knew Terry would never be able to make it, so he conceded that point and went on to rename the boy trying to leave the room. Once he had convinced himself of a new identity he would escape the kitchen but the routine was repeated at each new entrance and exit.

Unfortunately the dilemma followed through to additional routines. When he showered he could not stop scrubbing. When he washed his hair he could not stop washing. When he dried himself he could scarcely stop toweling. Fear had so completely immobilized his thinking that even the most simple task became a struggle.

In all my years of counseling I had never been confronted by such a baffling compulsion as the one

Terry possessed. Or which I should say possessed Terry. His *What If . . . ?* tape seemed totally indestructible. I knew I had to find a way to destroy it before it destroyed him. Our first necessity was to see that he recognized the strength of his fear. I didn't want him to fool himself on that score. Once he could recognize it for what it was, I knew that he would be able to talk to it. Again, to talk to it I felt it should have a name. We settled rather quickly on Mr. Spook. It seemed appropriate since it was the Halloween season.

I suggested that as he started out of one room into another he was to say, "Mr. Spook, you're losing your power. You're not as strong as you used to be. See how much faster I've gotten through the doorway tonight?"

Of course, even as I told him that, I knew his fear couldn't disappear in one try and probably not in a dozen. However, I also knew that if he would follow my instructions we were on our way.

Terry strived hard to break the pattern, but loosening the stranglehold of fear was easier said than done. There were times when he would backslide. I remember one particular incident when he had been tearing up some tile on the floor of an old home. As he took a tile to the rubbage bin out back, he couldn't let go. He stood there waving the tile in the air in an attempt to turn it loose, but his fingers gripped more tightly. Finally, on the verge of panic, he was able to challenge Mr. Spook and tell him to get lost. Almost immediately he began to calm down. He remembered that this was a familiar and known fear, and that he himself had named it. Therefore he, not the fear, was the master. So he began commanding Mr. Spook to move aside, and eventually he was able to drop the tile, shaken by the event, but another step closer to conquering the problem.

I think the day I began to breathe easier for him was the day I learned Terry had taken a trip to California to visit relatives. He had managed to spend not just one night but several away from home.

While I'm still on the subject of Terry, let me mention that he was also extremely shy. More than anything else he would have loved to have been a ladies' man but his conversations with them never progressed beyond a painful 'hello.'

Under hypnosis, I told Terry to visualize himself sitting in a streamlined dragster with a beautiful girl beside him. I could see that, even in a trance, he was enjoying the thought. Next I told him to see the vehicle moving and him the star driver of the day. I might explain that I used hypnosis because his fear was so deeply ingrained and intense. The thought of sitting in a high-powered dragster was his dream but he was shy with girls. In the trance I suggested he picture a beautiful girl sitting beside him, and visualize the thrill and power of the car speeding away. We had to condition his subconscious to this new image.

After a time we dropped hypnosis and dealt with the problem on a more routine level. Terry had to work hard to be free of his fear, but in time he was able to move out and live on his own, without Mr. Spook.

I cite the cases of Bill and Terry, which I assure you are not figments of my imagination, to illustrate the power and the grasp *What If . . . ?* tapes can have on a person's life.

One of the secrets of breaking up a fear tape is to accept the symptom by admitting its power and presence; then do the opposite of what the fear expects you to do, but do it in gradual steps and with humor. It is not always easy to convince another person to carry out some of the tasks I ask of them because they doubt if the suggestions will work and do not believe that their own thoughts are the real enemy. One way I'll ask a person to accept the symptom and practice it is illustrated by the woman who had allowed *What If . . . ?* tapes to run wild to the point that she could hardly go out to dinner with her husband. Her instructions were to buy a little jeweled pill box. When she was to go to dinner she was to symbolically place her fears in this little box. Before the meal was served she was to place the box on the table, and say to her husband and friends, "In this box are all my fears. They've plagued my life for so long that I thought if I treated them especially nice and took them out to dinner, maybe they might be nicer to me. If I open this lid up they'll all come out and I might faint or do something weird."

The point is this. She *admitted* she had the fears

and she took charge of the fear symptom instead of waiting for the fear to strike when it chose.

In the course of counseling she revealed her frustrations over trying to become pregnant for eight years and failing. When she talked about her job I realized how uptight it was making her. The following week I asked her husband to come with her so we could discuss her quitting that job and just hanging loose for a while. He fully agreed that his wife should quit work and plans were made for this. Three months later she stopped by my office to break the news to me that she was finally pregnant!

Did you ever wonder why you were told when you were afraid at night to whistle in the dark? If you whistle a happy tune your fear decreases. To aid a person in recognizing a decrease in fear, I use the concept of a fear thermometer from zero units of fear to one hundred units of fear which is panic time. During the course of therapy I will try to have him become aware of when he is able to notice a decrease in the units of fear in a disturbing situation. It is explained that I do not expect the fear to go from one hundred units to zero overnight, but since you have learned to be afraid you can also unlearn your fear. This helps the person have hope that someday soon he might be able to turn off his *What If . . . ?* tapes for good.

It is understandably difficult for a man to come into a doctor's office and say, "I'm impotent." The first few things I try to determine when confronted with this delicate situation is: (1) The man's work schedule (is he overworked and overfatigued?) (2) his drinking habits (does he drink to excess?), and (3) his fidelity (is he involved with another woman?).

The dynamics of the *What If . . . ?* tape are such that both the husband and the wife must understand the goal of breaking up the Impotency tape if it is to be accomplished. If he has experienced failure in attempting to make love to his wife, he begins to back off from future efforts, thinking, 'What If I fail again?' 'What will she think?' 'Maybe I'm getting too old.' 'What If I'm losing my potency.'

This is the time a wife might begin playing her Rejection tape. 'The reason he is impotent is that he doesn't love me anymore,' she may pout. She lets him know in subtle or not so subtle ways that this is her interpretation of his impotency and her attitude, in turn, places more pressure on the husband to perform.

He feels challenged. Not only is his masculinity at stake but he is faced with the additional task of proving he still cares. Sometimes a side effect of this vicious cycle is the husband turning to the solace of Scotch, Vodka, or whatever it takes to convince himself that if he's drunk he can't perform. Therefore, it has nothing to do with whether or not he cares about his wife; he is simply drunk. It's a cop out of course but often a husband will use it for as long as he can get away with it.

The Art Of Hanging Loose

The result is rather predictable; soon he can't, and even if he could she's so turned off by then that she wouldn't and on and on it goes, a giant windmill in their mind propelled by a common fuel—fear.

I asked a couple going through this traumatic experience to agree to follow to the letter some very basic instructions. In fact, the instructions are so simple they are deceiving. I explain that the real problem (assuming a physician's examination has eliminated any physical cause for the trouble) is fear of impotency itself. I tell the couple to make as their goal enjoying sexual foreplay and arousal without attempting to have intercourse. All I'm attempting to do at this stage is to bring their fear thermometer from one hundred units to zero.

There is no way it can be accomplished with one or two efforts so I have them agree to a specific time period—two weeks. For two weeks they are to go to bed at night and become reacquainted through touch, sensitivity and arousal. This almost always accomplishes the fear-reducing goal. Once the pressure is off the husband and he doesn't feel his masculinity is on the line he can respond to his wife more effectively.

If you're thinking of putting this technique into effect yourself, don't make the mistake made by a twenty-six-year-old man who came to me in desperation. He had been impotent with his wife, not once but twice. He was frantic. Very carefully I explained all of the various reasons for impotency in an otherwise healthy male and suggested he follow it to the letter. I told him the importance of touch and the philosophy of relaxation where sex is concerned, then I asked him to check back with me in fourteen days.

The next morning he called. "Doc," he moaned, "it didn't work."

"What didn't work?"

"I did all of the things you told me to do and I was impotent again."

"Look," I told him, "if you've got a hangup about throwing your money away and want to go on paying me without following my advice, go ahead. But if you want results, pay attention to what I'm saying. Two weeks."

"I didn't think that was important," he mumbled.

"It's the most important part," I said and hung up.

Two weeks later he came to see me. "You were right. We were able to go ahead and make love last night."

Some women also have a 'What If I Let Myself Go With My Sexual Feelings?' They are sure that something awful will happen to them. The feeling has been embedded and programmed into them that if they ever let themselves enjoy sexual relations with their husbands fully and completely, they would go completely out of control in their sexual lives. This is an unrealistic and irrational fear, but as long as they believe it they will enjoy the intimacy and love and passion of sex only to a point. Then, somehow, there is a silent click and it shuts off— because of the fear. 'If I let myself go I will become very immoral and impulsive in acting out my sexual behavior.'

A wife needs to be able to spot this kind of thinking and to challenge those thoughts. She should relax and say, 'Look, maybe that was Mom's hangup or Grandma's hangup, but it doesn't have to be mine. I can enjoy; I can be active, not passive, and enjoy sexual relations with my husband; I can hang loose and let go with him.' That is the greatest expression of love between man and woman—husband and wife. One other important aspect of this problem is for a woman to examine her own thinking to see how many resentments, hurts, and injustices she is holding on to in her mind: all the *Ain't Fair Blues* concerning her husband.

gin to think, "It ain't fair that I have to go to work; it ain't fair that it's Monday."

These powerful tapes can be extremely destructive. They not only stir up the blue feelings, in this case the depressed feelings, but also recall the memories of the past. Unfortunately, some people have an amazing ability to remember every bad experience, every insult, everything that someone did that wasn't nice or fair or right. They hold onto these old insults and injuries like they were prized possessions, and as they begin to play their *Ain't Fair Blues* tapes they soon can recall all these bad times and memories. Then they begin to feel lower and lower and more and more depressed.

I'm sure many husbands have discovered that their wives have an amazing capacity to recall, after twenty-some years of marriage, some event in time —the day, the hour and the moment—what you did that upset them, and how angry or hurt they were. Not only can they remember that event, but all the others. We poor men are baffled by women's amazing memories and their ability to hang onto this negative tape. The *Ain't Fair Blues* can also be played by a person who feels responsible for all that goes wrong around him. That person is like a blame blotter. If there is trouble he feels that it is all his fault and he'll take the blame. The blame and guilt it produces punishes him even more and he sinks lower and lower into his depression and self-pity. About the only thing productive about this tape is that it does allow the drug industry in America to sell millions of tranquilizers and anti-depressants to help elevate our moods or lift us out of the emotional pit this tape, this negative tape, has led us into.

Let's talk a little about depression. Believe it or not, depression is one of the most common of all ailments coming into any general physician's office, whether he recognizes it or not. It sometimes can be anger that is turned in on ourselves. We don't know how or have permission to deal with anger openly and honestly, so we turn it in on ourselves and thereby cut ourselves down. It is also seen as a result of the *Ain't Fair Blues* tape which is self-pity.

I'd like to make a distinction somewhere between the brooding over an *Ain't Fair Blues* tape, which leads to depression, and what it means to feel the despair of being a human who is alive with feelings. Despair sometimes is a result of the setbacks of life; the hurt and the pain and the frustrations; the agony of the loss of a loved one. We can feel that loss, but to be truly alive as a human being means to be truly aware. Aware of our feelings in the midst of the stresses of life; the defeats, the thrill of joy, of laughter, the release of crying, the feeling of pain and frustration, the warmth of love and the hurt of anger. We will feel all of these feelings.

I think there is one area that needs to be explored at this point. How do we come to terms with the reality of the death and grief experience? Death is a subject that is usually ignored, spoken in hushed terms, glossed over lightly or, in some extremes, denied its existence.

How to deal with grief is a subject that is seldom spoken of until we are in the midst of an experience of grief. Death always seems to come as a shock, even though we have consciously known and rationalized that it is the other side of the coin of life. A man is born and will also die someday, but when it strikes, very few are prepared to face the shock of the loss of a loved one.

Our friends and relatives come to bring us comfort and food, and to help us through this time of confusion and pain. Very often our friendly physician gives us medication so we won't feel the pain so much, and yet there are many decisions to be made.

The full impact of the death of a loved one usually hits a person by degrees. Thankfully, we are prevented from feeling the full impact of the shock all at once. People, struggling to express the right words to the bereaved, too often say the wrong things, but with good intentions.

For eleven years I was a Lutheran minister in California. I was involved in many tragic incidences with families when there was a death and a funeral to be planned. My most difficult tasks in administering to a family at a time of grief were not only in trying to help them come to terms with the grief reaction, but also in trying to undo the damage that was done by well-meaning friends and relatives as they tried, in their simple way, to give explanations and comfort as to why their loved one died. For instance, you often hear people say, "Well, cheer up, it's God's will." God wanted your son or your husband or your daughter. He caused the death, in essence.

There is a difference between God willing a death and God allowing a death. The same faction occurs when you buy a child roller skates. You're allowing him to have fun, but at the same time accepting the possibility that he might fall and skin his knees. However, it's a little different when the child is skating and you, all of a sudden, stick out your foot and trip him. That's causing him to be hurt. Perhaps some people can accept a death better if they feel that God caused it, but God does not go around filling babies with cancer or using drunks to kill families on the highways. His plan for man is not that man should kill himself or destroy the world in which he lives.

A most tragic story was told to me by a friend. She lost both her four-year-old and her five-year-old boys by drowning in a flood reserve, within a matter of minutes. She was so locked up with bitterness toward God and the world that it was nine years after the incident until I was finally able to talk with her. We began to talk about death and the "why" her boys died. She said someone had told her that God knew that her boys were beautiful and loving, and since God loves beautiful things, he picked them like flowers and took them with Him. She felt very angry at that point, at the thought of a God who would pick her two sons and take them when he had a whole universe of His own.

Someone else had tried to give her the comforting thought that God in His infinite wisdom probably knew that when her boys grew up they would probably do something terrible, perhaps criminal. In order to spare her that shame and pain He took them in their beautiful innocence. The idea of a demonic God who could both love and destroy at a capricious will is a schizophrenic God—one that I would have nothing to do with.

Very often in working through a grief experience you sense that a person feels that God took a loved one as punishment for their sins. During a seemingly normal birth of a fifth child, the mother was suddenly rushed to surgery. The baby's heart had stopped for some unknown reason. She was filled with much grief and also guilt. I was asked to visit her and I asked her the one question, "Do you feel that somehow you are being punished for your feelings about being pregnant at this time?"

She answered in the affirmative.

I told her I wasn't going to ask much that day but I did want her to think about another question, and then I'd see her in a couple of days. The question I asked her was, "If you were being punished, who died?"

Later she began to realize that if the baby had

never had a chance to live it was him who was punished, not her. How often, when a loved one dies there is enough guilt in each of us that we somehow feel it's our fault. Maybe I should have done this or that. We want to blame ourselves and we want to feel that God is punishing us for our feelings about them.

Another common explanation of why someone died is that it was fate. Your number is up when your number is up. It's almost as if God had some kind of whimsical way of deciding that on such and such a day in June at eleven o'clock a person would die from falling in the bathroom. Why? Because he just thought it would be nice to fall? There is nothing that you could do to forestall your fate. This is a very common belief held during war times and men will talk about a bullet having your number on it or not having your number on it. A God of fate is again a God of a very strange behavior who could not be a loving God as we are told.

I think you must understand at this point that what I am talking about is coming out of my own personal experiences and my own faith. The grief process sometimes is so covered up by the activity and the medication that one does not really feel the impact of the loss of the significant loved one until about three weeks after the funeral. Then the loneliness, the pain and the despair become stark reality.

But to whom can you turn at that time? Your

friends have told you how well you did; your relatives were so proud of you, how you took it so bravely. You were able to manage yourself beautifully, and you didn't break down and fall apart. And if you mention your feelings to friends, they say, "Well, we thought you were over that. Now pull yourself together!"

This is the time when there is the need for someone to listen to you, to feel with you; maybe not trying to answer every question but just letting you know that they understand; that they know it hurts.

There are grief reactions which are so powerful that I have been puzzled by the persons' inability to finish the grief process and resume a more normal living pattern. The problem often is resolved when I realize that the grieving person has to finally say 'good-by' to the loved one. For this person there is a certain part of them that will not let them finish grieving over the loss of the loved one. After a period of time I may discover that the police widow has not told me of the room where she still keeps her former husband's uniforms and other personal articles; how she can't go into the room and decide what to keep and what to dispose of because it would mean she finally had to say 'good-by'. For her to accomplish this task is the key to completing her grief process.

Several years ago I counseled with a family; in particular with the mother over the horrible grief reaction caused by the senseless murder of her daughter in the desert. The long trial and the first

Christmas without her in the home kept the bitterness and hate tapes very active. After Christmas the mother discovered the key to allow her to finally say good-by to her beloved daughter. She had to visit the place where her daughter was murdered and have a mental picture of the area before she would say 'good-by'. I called the police and the district attorney who had been so wonderful to the family. With the police and the district attorney, the mother went to the spot in the desert where her girl had died. It worked. The mother called me and told me that now she could let go; that this place in the desert was truly beautiful. On the spot where she was found she planted wild flowers that would bloom again and again every spring.

I also think that very often we handle children poorly at times of death. It begins with the prayer that we all learned as children.

> ... "Now I lay me down to sleep.
> I pray the Lord my soul to keep.
> If I should die before I wake.
> I pray the Lord my soul to take."

That prayer alone is enough to frighten a child if he listens to the words. When there is a funeral, there are emotional reactions that need to be expressed and questions that need to be answered as honestly as possible for the child. They are so often dodged or ignored, and sometimes the young person is sent away to another relative while all the funeral preparation and the service take place. The child is left with puzzlement, bewilderment, a need to cry and a need to grieve. However, no one seems to allow him to feel his normal pain and grief, and then to express it.

Very often, if this grief experience is not worked through with the child, he will express his depression in a different manner than the way adults experience depression. A child can strike out at the world; teachers, friends and family. His acting-out behavior is often labeled as delinquent behavior and incorrigibility. Unfortunately, we miss the point that this behavior is his striking-out at life because he feels robbed; he feels cheated; he feels alone, and he has some pain and depression to work through.

Some people have gone through one tragedy after another and always seem to be able to smile through it and be strong. This brings to mind one such person I have counseled. One day I couldn't help but notice that there was always a trace of a tear in each eye, even though a smile tried to hide the tears that needed to be shed. I asked this woman to tell me about the people in her life who have died. Then she began to tell me a story leading back to World War II and the Japanese prison camps. I asked her what she did when a loved one died. She said she had to take care of the arrangements and see to this and that. I said, "When did you cry? When did you grieve?"

"Well, I never had time." This became a pattern, and her life had been unduly filled with tragedy.

And each time I asked her, "And when did you cry? When did you grieve?"

"Well, somebody had to take care of details and I never got around to it. I never had time."

I told her I thought it was time she cried and grieved for all the loved ones that she never found the time for before. She said she just couldn't cry for them now.

I told her, "Yes, you can. I'll give you permission to cry and release the grief you have stored up in your heart and body. I want you to tell your husband to hold you tight; that you're going to cry all night long and sob the deep sobs you've kept deep inside your heart?"

"You can't just do that," she said.

"Well, this is Tuesday, how about tonight?"

And typically on cue she said, "Well, I'm sure I can't do it tonight. I don't have time tonight. Maybe Thursday night I could cry."

I gave her the very strange wording, "but remember, I have given you *permission* to cry for all the loved ones you have lost and have never had the time to cry for. Don't think about it; just wonder about how it will feel to finally be able to cry and grieve and mourn, and to let go of the pain."

The next week she came back and I asked her, "Well, how did it go on Thursday night when you cried?"

"You rascal, you knew I couldn't wait until Thursday night. That night when I went to bed I told my husband to hold me tight, that I had to cry all night long."

I'd like to share with you my own personal outlook and philosophy about life and death. Remember, this is my *own personal view,* and as a philosopher of old once said, "Each bird must whistle through his own beak." This is just one person expressing his views and his beliefs about death and life. I started out this chapter saying that we play a tape called "It Ain't Fair", but the truth of the matter is that there isn't a balanced wheel of justice operating in life. Very often life *isn't* fair and that's a fact. It isn't fair that a six week old baby develop a cancerous tumor. It isn't fair that we were born in the United States of America, *per se,* and not in the deepest jungles of Africa or 'out back' in Australia —that isn't fair. It isn't fair that we were born with a healthy body instead of a deformed body. That isn't fair either.

There are many things in life that just aren't fair, but they are facts of life. The fact that there is death —that is a fact! As long as we live there is always the reality that death could come at any time. And it will come sometimes at a most inopportune time and we can say, "It isn't fair." Death then isn't fair, but it is a fact, and not a negative tape, unless we begin to brood over it, dwell on the death of a loved one and not emotionally and psychologically let go of them.

I have often replied to the question, 'Why did my loved one die?' by asking what the death certificate said. Was the cause of death cancer . . . emphysema . . . or a heart attack? These are the reasons for the death. The fact of the death is that we are vulnerable, that we are human.

I have my own personal view as a Christian. I see God and man both viewing death as a mutual enemy that must be destroyed. I see the birth of Christ—His coming into the world—and His death on a cross, as God doing something personally. He allowed Christ to die and enter the nothingness of death, and then to defeat death on its own terms with the Easter morning victory of life over death— the resurrection of Jesus. This is my own personal statement of faith.

When I was a minister and someone asked me, "Why didn't God do something for my loved one when I prayed for them?" I said, "He did, about two thousand years ago. He so loved the world that He gave his only begotten Son."

Death, then, in my point of view is not the handmaiden of God but the enemy of God, the enemy of man that will be destroyed. My faith is in the God who created life, who raised Christ from the dead and who has promised us that same resurrection and victory over death. Instead of saying to a person that it was God's will or that God took your loved one, I'd rather share with a person a God who knows what it is to grieve and lose a son, to offer a son to a very painful death on a cross that truly "wasn't fair".

so. Once you have made a mistake, once you have goofed, you are not perfect. And when the other person has made a mistake in life, he isn't perfect either.

Getting all uptight about *you* not being perfect, or *them* not being perfect and demanding perfection is the impossible task and dream. It's like demanding that the sun rise in the west instead of the east because you're tired of it always coming up in the same spot. The perfectionist is the person who gets 98 out of 100 on a test and then complains to his friends for two weeks that he shouldn't have missed those other two questions. How terrible it was of him! How stupid it was! He completely ignores the fact that 98 out of 100 is still an *A*.

The perfectionist always has a feeling that people should be able to live up to his expectations and to read his mind; to think his thoughts and always be there, ready to meet his every need. He becomes very hard on himself. The tragedy is that a perfectionistic person feels deep-down that only if he's perfect can he accept himself and will others accept him. Thus, by demanding perfection in himself and others, he does a beautiful job of making people fear him and dislike him. This doesn't mean that a person should not be productive or creative, or set goals in life. It does mean that you come to terms with your limitations and the world's limitations and accept them as they are. Accept yourself just as you are, and then take the potential that is there and let it grow. Learn how to forgive others when you practice the art of self-forgiveness.

A perfectionist can also be the strong, silent type who holds in all the irritations of other people's mistakes, but who can't talk about them at that time. He keeps thinking about them and brooding about them. Finally, a week or ten days later, some other little thing goes wrong and then he explodes like an erupting volcano causing others to look around and say, "What was that all about?" The person who exploded also knows he over-reacted and made a fool of himself.

We then proceed to the next tape which is the *Name Calling* tape. When you've really blown it, you proceed to talk about how stupid you were. "What was the matter with you?" "Why did you have such a rage?" You call yourself dirty names—stupid dumb bunny, hothead, *et cetera*. It's another way of being uptight and feeling very miserable.

This type of person also seems to feel that life is grim. Even when he tries to play, it becomes a contest or war and he can't hang loose and just have fun. He always feels that he must compete and prove himself just one more time.

The driven perfectionist may make all kinds of goals so he may be driven to achieve this and achieve that, but the joy of achieving is never quite reached. When he reaches his goal he says, to his dismay, "I'm here. Why don't I feel better about it?" Then he trys harder next time for the impossible dream which turns out to be the nightmare of the negative tape of the perfectionist.

A very fine engineer was brought by his wife for therapy. He admitted he needed help and wanted to change. When he was performing and problem-solving as an engineer he was like a great computer sorting out the facts. However, when it came to his relationship with people at work or at home he was either a demanding, authoritarian dictator, or he would explode and have a tantrum like a child when he didn't get his way.

He was eager to learn about his negative tapes and how he could turn them off. He realized he could set himself up for the day by what he started to think about before breakfast. One morning he reported that as he was shaving he could hear his negative tapes start, and he followed my instructions. He looked into the mirror and contemplated God's good sense of humor in creating him. Then he said to himself, "Hang loose. Turn off the old tapes." He said it worked. He could feel himself relax.

During the work day I asked him to stop at periodic times to listen to what was going on inside his head and decide if he liked what he heard. I also believe in giving people homework between appointments, so I had instructed him to praise his co-workers more and watch their reactions. He complimented two of his fine foremen and said they almost died of shock. This engineer is having a lot of fun learning the art of hanging loose at last.

5

How to Turn Off the Negative Tapes and Hang Loose

One of the major mistakes in the field of mental health is that too much effort is spent in testing and giving people exotic diagnostic labels. These labels not only pigeonhole people, but with the label comes the feeling of hopelessness and despair. Mental illness itself implies a disease model which says that the person is not responsible for his problems. We have also lived with the myth that once origin of the problem is discovered causing a person's emotional illness, then that insight is supposed to be curative. But too often people have the wonderful perceptivity but flounder as to where they go from here with the insight. I have seen people change and have never discovered the underlying cause. Curiously, after a person has changed he will often have great understanding of the causes of his problem. I also believe that a long passive regression into the past of a person in psychotherapy serves as a barrier which forestalls learning how to live more successfully in the here and now. I believe people can change, and some can change rather miraculously. Change is not something someone else can do for you. You must assume personal responsibility for changing. Decide what it is you want to change and then examine all the barriers and resistance that exist in the path of your change. Be ready to pay the price and to work hard. In this chapter I'll discuss ways of changing and growing as a person. The following subtitles will offer some ideas as to what is to follow.

1. Talk yourself out of trouble.
2. The power of key words or phrases in breaking up negative tapes.
3. Decide who is going to be in charge of your emotional life.
4. The power of laughter in hanging loose.
5. Climbing out of a rut and learning new behavior.
6. How to unwind and go to sleep naturally.
7. The power of belief about self.

1. TALK YOURSELF OUT OF TROUBLE.

The first step in breaking up or turning off a negative tape is to listen for the negative thoughts as soon as they have started. This can be difficult at first because negative tapes are habitual thoughts which often are going on because you are thinking about or listening for the tapes. Remember, so many of us blame others and the world for how we feel that it is painful to believe that "you are your own bummer." Negative tapes cannot be turned off by just ignoring them or pretending them away. If you can learn to spot the negative tape when it first starts, then you won't have to experience all the painful emotions and bad memories that would result if the negative tapes are allowed to run their destructive course. Negative tapes that are interrupted can make a person feel so low he has to reach up to touch bottom.

Now once a negative tape is going you must challenge these thoughts by actually talking to yourself to interrupt and turn them off. Remember how Ann broke up her *What If . . . ?* tape by challenging the thoughts with another dialogue about her admitting to herself that she was the world's greatest vomiter? The important thing to remember is that you find what things you can say to yourself that will break up a negative tape. This is important. You must believe that you have to challenge these tapes. Break them apart—destroy them—interrupt them. No matter how you do it you can either say, "Turn it off. I don't want to listen to that garbage any more. I have let too much of my life be ruined by self-pity to have it happen again," or "Get out of here, don't bug me again." Whatever it is you begin to challenge; you begin to say things inside your head to turn them off. Remember the girl who had to say to herself, "I'm the world's greatest vomiter!" This is how she began to talk to herself in order to break up that very powerful *What If* tape.

2. THE POWER OF KEY WORDS IN BREAKING UP NEGATIVE TAPES

The champion of all negative tape players was a man in his fifties, unemployed, who came for counseling. He started off saying, "I hear you are a pretty good psychologist." It always worries me when someone tells me I'm good, because I have a feeling that a game is about to begin. 'You be the great doctor and I'll be the great patient.' I have a philosophy that I don't have any patients in my practice, just people. I began to explain to him my philosophy of needing to know if he wanted to change and his responsibility for his change.

Through our conversations I began to realize that this was a very brilliant man, that he had read more books on more subjects than I had ever thought of reading in ten lifetimes. I suddenly began to realize that I was coming up very short, knowledgewise, when he asked if I had read this book or that book and I kept saying, "No, I haven't read that book." "No, I'm not familiar with that author's work," and "No, I'm not acquainted in that field."

Finally, in desperation, I said, "Look, John, would you go home and write down all the areas of interest in your life. Tell me how many years you have been interested in them, and we'll see what we can find that will be a key for your life now so you can get started in a new career."

The following week he returned to the office with a list that went from astrology to zoology. It looked like a college catalog. I could not help but be puzzled now, even more, that this man had so much knowledge, and had spent so many years preparing himself and becoming so well rounded. I said, "Tell me what the major instruction or advice your mother gave you?"

He said, "I thought of that. She said 'Always be prepared'."

So I said, "I guess you spent fifty-seven years preparing yourself, but she never gave you permission to start. Am I correct?"

He nodded and said he'd never had permission to go.

"In fact," I said, "you had such self-doubts that probably when you were working on a project, a little frown would shut you down."

"It did, it did."

Then we got into the concept of negative tapes and he said, "Boy, I'm the world's champ." He began to realize with his agile mind that his own thinking was his greatest enemy.

Now, something else fell into place. For the sake of delicacy of writing I will choose socially acceptable terms. John had a recurring dream that had bothered him all his life. This was his dream. He was forever having to go to the bathroom in a public place, and every time he entered the men's restrooms, the urinals and toilets were filled with human waste, and so was he. "Now in dream interpretation," he said, "I understand that you are to see yourself in the dream. What it's saying I'm full of a lot of waste. I'm the toilet, and I'm full of a lot of waste."

I asked him, "Then to make a toilet work, what must you do to it?"

He said, "Flush it."

"Right," I said.

He realized he'd been carrying all this junk around inside his head; all his negative tapes had been showing up in his recurring dreams; and the thing that he needed to do was to learn how to "flush it" with his negative tapes. Above his toilet he wrote this sign to remind him every morning to be physically and emotionally clean, "Flush it!"

3. DECIDE WHO IS GOING TO BE IN CHARGE OF YOUR EMOTIONAL LIFE

An important step in breaking up or turning off negative tapes is for the individual to make a decision by asking himself, "Do I want to go on feeling this way? How long do I want to feel miserable?"

One young executive approached the problem in a very businesslike manner. He said, "I know I have these negative tapes, so I'm going to get rid of them. When I start doing my negative tapes I give myself ten minutes, and say, 'OK, I'll give you ten minutes, but after that time I'm turning you off because I have to go on with the day'."

You can also make a decision like this when someone says something very nasty or hurtful, or tries to push your anger button or your guilt button. Instead of just reacting to those around you, where they can press your button and you respond, say to yourself, "Do I want to get hungup on their hangups?" You can make that decision. You can begin to realize that they are human beings with faults. Funny things are wrong with them, like you and me. Instead of being upset when you see that they have problems, say to yourself, "That's their problem, I don't have to make it mine."

Look at the amount of destructive energy that is wasted by hate. The *Hate* tape is a very destructive one. *Hate is a means by which we punish and destroy ourselves for the actions of others.*

One time a young teenage girl came in for therapy and was very upset. She said, "I *hate* my teacher. I can't stand her." On and on she went.

"Wait a minute," I said. "Is your teacher in the room now?"

"No, she's not here now, Doc. That's a crazy question."

"Here you are in my office, and here we always have a good time talking. Right? But you're all upset and you're getting more and more agitated.

The more you think about that teacher, the more you hate her. If she's the enemy, why do you allow her to spoil your day today? Why do you allow her the privilege of coming into your head, stirring up your mind and churning your stomach, getting you all upset? You can make a decision about that. You don't have to have her ruining your day when you're not even in her classroom?"

4. THE POWER OF LAUGHTER IN HANGING LOOSE

Laughter is such a marvelous tool to help us hang loose. If we could learn to laugh at ourselves more, laugh at the world and not be so uptight, it would be great. There is a real healing power in laughter. We enjoy a good comedian because he can make us forget, make us relax and feel like life is worth living again. As you can tell by now, I use laughter quite a bit as a healing force.

One day an eleven-year-old girl came from class to see about a problem with her music teacher. She was a bright little girl and quite shy.

I said, "You're doing well in your subjects?"

"Oh, yes, I do very well, but the music teacher is just frightening me to death, and I just know I'm going to fail. I'm terrified of this man."

"Tell me about him."

"Would you believe he's an ex-marine drill sergeant? He's a big guy with a paunch. He must feel we're still his raw recruits, the way he storms around and shouts at us. He says, 'All right, who wrote this?' and points his finger at you. I just choke up and stutter and stammer, and he chews me out for being so stupid. I can't think of anything to say and I'm always worrying about when he's going to call on me, or when he'll get mad and embarrass me. Can you help me?"

"Well, I think so. Now this is our secret. On Monday morning when you go back to class I want you to work on having this picture in your mind of the teacher. I want you to see this great, big ex-marine drill sergeant with a paunch, walking around the room and blustering; but picture him dressed only in red, long-handled underwear that is two sizes too big, with the flap down at the back."

She smiled, then giggled, and said, "I think I'll try that." And she did.

The next week when she came back I asked her how everything was going, and she told me, "It worked, it worked! I'm not frightened any more because I see him walking around just like you said." She was beginning to relax and enjoy the class again and not to be so fearful. She could laugh when she told me about it.

A couple of weeks went by, and when she returned she said, "Doc, I think I'm in trouble."

I asked, "Why?"

She said, "As I was leaving the class he asked if he could see me for a minute. He said he had noticed that for the past several weeks I was always looking at him with a little smile on my face. It really puzzled him."

I asked her what she did, and she told me that she had related to him what I had told her to do. I was curious as to how he reacted.

She said, "At first he laughed, but then he became horrified and wanted to know if I had told any of the other students what I saw when I looked at him. I assured him that I hadn't."

Can you imagine, though, what happened to him every time he looked at that little girl and saw her smiling face? Now he knew what she was smiling at when she looked at him. He had to change.

I know sometimes we get so uptight with our own self-worth and importance that perhaps it does us good to go into the bathroom and shut the door, look in the mirror and contemplate God's good sense of humor in creating us.

We have become experts at emotionally building catastrophes out of small things; always being uptight and angry at everyone. We get upset at things we can't change, and probably not upset enough at things we should change. Hawaiians have a beautiful philosophy summarized in the song, *Ain't No Big Thing Brother,* by Kui Lee.

In the consulting that I do in dentistry, one of my big tasks is to help the dentist and his staff better understand the uptight patient who enters the office filled with fears, anxieties, and playing his own version of his tape, "I Hate Dentists". The patient will say to the dentist, "I hate dentists, but not you personally." The dental office is a pressure atmosphere filled with frustration, anger, hostility, and fear. Without becoming aware of these pressures, the people working in the office can be caught up in the negative atmosphere and then take it out on each other. Sometimes the dentist gets a little carried away with the Doctor Degree and soon there is an uptight office.

I tell them a story to help them hang loose. It was told to me by a Jewish friend and I love to relate it. My friend said she had gone back to her 25th high school reunion. She hadn't seen her best friend for years.

Sarah came up to her, embraced her, hugged her and said, "Amy, how have you been?"

"Just fine, and it's so good to see you. How has the world been treating you, Sarah?"

"Would you believe that when Harry and I got married he took me on a honeymoon—three months in the Mediterranean, and a month in Israel? What do you think of that?"

"Fantastic!" Amy said.

"We came back home and he showed me the new home that he bought for me—sixteen rooms; a new Mercedes. What do you think of that, Amy?"

"Fantastic!"

"And now for our 20th Anniversary, he gave me a diamond ring—ten carats!"

"Fantastic!"

"And now after the reunion we're going to go on a cruise around the world. What do you think of that?"

"Oh, that's fantastic!"

"Oh, Amy, I've been talking so fast about what Harry's done for me, I forgot to ask what your Abe has done for you?"

"Oh, we've had a good life together."

"But what has he done special?"

"Well, let's see. What has he done special? He did one thing real special for me."

"What's that?"

"He sent me to charm school."

"Sent you to charm school? What did you go to charm school for."

"To teach me how to say 'Fantastic' instead of 'Bullshit'."

The purpose of this story is to give an office a powerful word to help them hang loose—anything to break the tension. Some offices, after hearing this joke, have sewn the word 'Fantastic' on the under side of their collars. When someone gets uptight a member of the staff just lifts the collar.

5. CLIMBING OUT OF A RUT AND LEARNING NEW BEHAVIOR.

Realize that when you are learning new behavior you'll flounder for a time because you have to *think* about what you're doing. Don't call yourself a "phony" for floundering. It's just simply new behavior and that's the way people act when they're learning how to do new things.

For instance, if a person is very shy, and you ask him to try to greet two or three new people a day, just asking them small things, like "How do you feel about that?" he'll often tell you, "But I don't feel like doing that. It makes me so uncomfortable. It's so hard to do."

I tell him that it's doing the hard things that get us out of the rut. Nobody will know that you are trying new behavior. It's like learning how to ski. When you take lessons, the first thing they teach you is how to fall. Then the next thing they teach you is how to fill up the hole left in the snow where you fell. And as you're there—scrambling around, trying to stand up, falling down, getting up, filling up the hole—you feel very clumsy. You don't call yourself a phony, because that is normal behavior for people learning how to ski. And then you see some little nine-year-old kid come swishing by saying, "Hi, mister! Having trouble?" You get so infuriated because he skis so effortlessly, without thinking. He just glides down the mountainside, and there you are, tangled up in ski poles and snow, feeling so awkward. But that's normal behavior when you're learning how to ski.

Let's take the everyday housewife—caught up in her depression, in her blues. She's gained a little too much weight. She feels that life isn't fair. The kids get up, hustle for themselves and get off to school.

The Art Of Hanging Loose

When her husband's gone to work, she staggers out in her pajamas, pulls herself up to the kitchen table, pours herself a cup of coffee and has a cigarette. She looks at the dishes in the sink, and the dirt on the floor. She looks around the family room and sees clothes that haven't been put away, newspapers on the floor, ash trays not emptied and she begins to feel more depressed than ever before so she turns on another soap opera. This helps her feel more depressed and she'll say, "I can't change until I feel like changing. I feel so depressed I don't feel like possibly doing anything different."

If you waited until you *felt* like doing something different you'd stay in a rut for a long time. I ask people, "Do you want to change and stop being depressed?" If you do, you'll have to do things when you don't feel like doing them. First, look at the messages within your house. Everything is saying something to you—that you're no good, that you're a lousy housewife, that you're a bad wife, an incompetent mother, you're a slob. Be depressed! But then you say, 'I don't *feel* like cleaning up the house.' Well, who said you had to *feel* like doing it! Everything in that environment is a message which is saying 'be depressed'. Your cleaning the house is a way of saying, 'I'm wiping out that message.' This is one way to begin to break out of the blues. Remember, you *don't have to feel like doing it,* but you will find, in time, a sense of self-pride.

How else do you want to learn to hang loose? One

of the deadliest things of all is developing a dull habit, a dull way of approach to life. It's called a rut. To get out of it, do some things, make some decisions. What will I do differently this week or this month to break out of the rut, to avoid being mesmerized by the television, of just living that same old routine? If you've wanted to play a musical instrument—then why not try? If you wanted to do this or do that—if it makes you feel better about yourself—why not try? Give yourself permission to say, "Why not?" You'd be surprised at how often we repeat the pattern of the past. If we have had parents who always felt that hard work was the only thing to do, and never learned how to have fun, somehow we get the message that we aren't supposed to have fun and relax.

6. HOW TO UNWIND AND GO TO SLEEP NATURALLY

Symptomatic of our uptightness is the sheer amount of sleeping pills the American public swallows each night, hoping to sleep. Isn't it strange a baby doesn't have to think about going to sleep when it's tired. It just goes to sleep. When we become older we worry about sleeping. We have to think about it, and we find it is our thinking about sleep, and all the other things running wild through our minds, that prevents us from relaxing and just drifting off into dreamland.

There are several ways that are helpful in breaking the routine of being uptight, suggestions that people have used successfully in learning how to relax and sleep.

One method has been to relax every muscle in your body, starting with your toes. Tighten and hold the tension in each muscle, and then let go. When you let go, picture each muscle fiber unwinding until you have gone through and relaxed every muscle, including your face, jaw, eyes, neck, shoulders, and arms. It is incredible the amount of tension we carry around, just in our muscles. However, we cannot make the body respond just by saying "Let go," but it will understand when we know what it is to feel the tension of the muscles, and then the relaxed muscles. Practice this and it will help break up the bad habit of sleeplessness.

For some people who have chronic insomnia I have used another interesting technique. One woman who had complained of being an insomniac most of her life said she could not sleep without the aid of alcohol or sleeping pills. I asked her what one thing about housework she hated the most. She answered, without question, that it was ironing. She told me that she just hated it, loathed it and put it off. I said, that as long as she couldn't sleep at night, why ruin the day by thinking about ironing? When she went home tonight and *knew* that she wasn't going to sleep, she might as well iron all night and at least be productive. She went home, got out the ironing board and started ironing. She got so angry that she would do anything to get out of it, even going to sleep, and that she did.

I used the same technique with a man. I asked him what kind of task around the house he hated the most. This one said it was waxing the floors. So I said to him that he might as well have a clean house and wax the floors at night. And he went home and waxed the floors way into the night thinking, "Gee, this is kind of dumb. Here I am waxing these floors when I could be in bed sleeping." Whereupon he went to bed and slept.

Another technique that has been most helpful in learning how to relax has been through the use of self-hypnosis. There are some good books on this which will help you relax and be able to enjoy a very calm and peaceful sleep. If you notice, however, as you are lying in bed that there are many thoughts running around in your mind, and tasks that you would like to accomplish, get out of bed. Go into another room and write down everything that you have on your mind—all the things that you are concerned about. It helps drain off the mental energy of the thinking process by writing these thoughts down on paper and then leave the paper in the other room. In the morning you can re-evaluate your list to see what can be changed and what can't be changed. Then ask yourself, "Am I procrastinating again? Is this what's really bugging me. What am I procrastinating most about?" When you decide what needs to be done first, make a decision that this is the first thing you will do that day. When we know there are some things we must do, until we complete that task, some of that tension will remain with us.

7. THE POWER OF BELIEFS ABOUT SELF

When we consider that a baby is born into this world not only as a natural being, but enters this world most of the time with lots of love, hugging, kissing and laughing. This helps the baby to learn and grow at a very rapid rate. An infant loves to touch, taste, move, crawl, to use his arms, kick his legs, and becomes fascinated with his fingers. A young child is naturally stoned on life. Everything is wonderful and a mystery and a child will ask a thousand 'Why?'s. He explores the world by climbing, looking, and questioning.

He learns at an incredible rate and he discovers how to read the non-verbal cues given to him by his family members. Children are very perceptive as they read our non-verbal cues. In fact a child psychologist is a kid who understands his parents. The mystery and the awe of the learning process make life exciting for the child. It's unbelievable when you think that by the time a child goes into first grade he has learned the difficult art of manipulation of symbols—symbolic language; learned the rudiments, and perfected quite a few of them, of being able to get along socially, not only at home but with other people. He has learned so many "first learning experiences" that it's extraordinary. In fact, I doubt if a child in the first six years will ever learn as many new things the rest of his life as he does at that time.

And then something strange happens. I know this may sound exaggerated, but too often when a child goes to school he gets the message loud and clear to "Sit down, shut up, don't talk, don't touch. Now we are going to teach you something." A little kid probably feels "That's funny. I thought I was learning all along."

But what he does learn is that now learning is not for learning's sake and for the sake of curiosity. Now when he learns it is to get a grade. He discovers that everyone is ranked from high to low. Even parents get upset when they discover their child is only average. You can almost hear a parent saying in an exaggerated form, "Son, your mother and I are both average, we know that, but we are going to break the family tradition. You will be a genius whether you have it or not."

So a child begins to feel the pressure of competition; of being graded; of making mistakes. That's funny because before he went to school, when he was learning something new, he made mistakes and this didn't make him a failure. He was just learning how to do something. He was learning how to tie his shoe, for example. He sat there and fumbled for a while with the shoe strings, struggling with the fingers and the loops, and finally he decided, "Aw, shucks, I can't get it. They'll just flop awhile." He doesn't feel that he is a failure at that time. He just figures he hasn't learned how to tie his shoe laces. Someday he will, maybe.

Now a child is beginning to learn that not making a mistake determines how he is going to be accepted and approved and loved and rewarded. So he feels like he is chasing the eternal carrot. Learning becomes something that you manipulate and reward from externals, by grade, dollars, etc. It's sad because children, as they grow, find the inner joy of learning is turned off. By the time some of them reach the 5th grade you look at a classroom and you can see those who have been bored out or conditioned out of learning for the sake of learning. School has become a drag. It too often is the place where a person begins to believe he is no good.

The more I work with people, the more I am amazed at their complexities. More and more I realize that it is not so much the one or two traumatic events in a person's life that are significant, but rather the insignificant ones that you may not ever hear verbally. It's the feelings that you receive about yourself that create self-doubt. It's the messages you receive about yourself, not just once but repeated constantly, that make you begin to develop certain beliefs about your world, about people, about yourself. There's real power in what we believe. The power of your beliefs can be that which sets you free, or that which locks you in your own prison.

Someone once asked Thomas Edison, "It must

have been awful to have failed a thousand times before you made a successful electric light bulb."

He showed his secret of hanging loose when he answered by saying, "Well, I never considered them failures. I just figured I found a thousand ways not to make a light bulb."

How many of you would have stayed with a task that long? Or would you have copped out at ten or twelve failures and said, "Well, I can't do it." If you said you couldn't do it and believed it, you wouldn't. The word "can't" is very interesting. In itself it's just a symbol. But if you begin to believe it and give it substance, it becomes reality in your own life. This reality is a very powerful force in stopping you.

Somehow as a person grows he is bombarded by self-doubts from people who are always looking at the negatives. You may get three A's, two B's and a C, and a parent will say, "How did you get a C?" People are often more comfortable in talking about their faults and other people's faults than in what's good about ourselves and others. An important aspect of learning how to set yourselves free is to honestly cut yourself free from the self-doubts, those imprisoning fears and beliefs from the past that you carry around like a ball and chain. Make peace with your past and come to terms with the *who* that you are in *the here and the now*. Realize that none of us is perfect, but you are a lot better than you believe. Maybe you can accept yourself and then develop that which is in you to really grow. Yes, we are sometimes our cruelest jury, judge, and executioner. No wonder you are so uptight.

As the title to Jess Lair's book suggests, *I Ain't Much Baby, But I'm All I've Got,* you have to be able to decide, "I don't have to prove to myself again and again every day that I'm worthwhile." You discover that you can accept yourselves as you are. Then you can change. Someone once said to me, "I had better love me, in case nobody else does." Jesus even said it, "Love thy neighbor as thyself." It means that we will have nothing to give to another until we have first been able to accept and love ourselves as we are.

6

Marriage — the First Fifty Years Are the Hardest

This chapter will not be an in-depth study of the social and psychological ramifications of the stability versus the instability of the institution of marriage in America, with all of its foibles and failings. It will give some observations and suggestions on how to help unwind uptight marriages in order that partners may enjoy each other more fully than they ever dreamed possible.

One of the interesting questions I ask a couple who come in for counseling is, "How did you two happen to get married?" The various answers are always surprising. We would usually suspect that choosing a marital partner "till death do us part, for better or for worse," (even if it's worse than we thought) would involve far more rational reasoning and selection. According to divorce statistics, we could say that perhaps we don't do too well in choosing a mate. It has been in vogue as of late for some people to revolt against the piece of paper called the marriage contract, or marriage license. They feel it really isn't important. But day after day and year after year we wonder about the nature of our commitment to the relationship; the *who* that we are and how we are both changing.

We might even explore, with professional help, some of the hidden reasons why and how we selected the person to fit our needs, our hidden agenda, or as I phrase it, our psychological marriage contract. I fully realize that in this short space of time we could in no way cover all of the possible psychological marriage contracts. Nor could we describe all the reasons in our hidden agenda of how we select the person we marry.

I'd like to point out that not all selection processes are negative, even though many of my examples on the following pages might seem to be stating that we always select for the wrong reasons. The psychological contract is basically this: we have a felt need and we look for a person to help fill that need.

This kind of programming comes from the past and is very often outside of our awareness and yet it can sometimes have marvelous results. There are occasions when you can need another person and, in the ensuing discovery of each other, find a rareness and a quality of openness, honesty, and intimacy that has never quite existed with another person. You enjoy the laughter and fun, and don't have to think about what to say or how to say it. It's as if you have found someone who says, "I need somebody to trust me and be open with me," and you say, "Me, too! Isn't it great that out of all the world, you and I met." So we do know that there are many positive psychological needs and contracts that are consummated.

A few years ago, a young couple came to me for counseling. They had been married for seven years. When I asked them why they were there, they told me that they didn't know whether to get a divorce or not. I asked them how they met and how they decided to choose each other for marriage. Their answer was very frank. "We met; we had a moment of exchange, and out of that exchange and brief meeting came a pregnancy."

The more I studied them, wondered and listened to their problems, I noticed that something was lacking. I said, "Wait a minute, what is your psychological marriage contract? Not the contract written on paper, but what kind of philosophy or beliefs do you both have about people who have to get married?"

As we continued the discussion, it was brought to light that they both had this hidden agenda: "People who have to get married can never love one another"—whatever that means. With that belief they could never really have, or enjoy, or discover, a very deep communicative relationship and have fun together. During the discussion it was discovered that they looked upon love as some starry-eyed, explosive, sky-rocketing feeling.

I asked them if they thought they could tear up that original contract and if they'd like to work towards establishing a new one. I explained that we would not worry about the fact that they had to get married. If they'd do some exploration, they could build the quality of a communicative relationship where one could listen and hear the other, enjoy the other, and be intimate with the other. Once they established that depth of communication we could even say that it would be a loving relationship. They had never thought of it that way, so they decided to tear up their old contract and write a new one.

There's so much talk these days about marriage being just a piece of paper. I don't know about you, but I've been married for over twenty-three years. It seems like yesterday—and you know what a terrible day yesterday was! Seriously, how many of us have ever gone to our safety deposit box and pulled out our Marriage Certificate. The paper isn't the issue at all. The fear that is confronting us is that of a commitment to an intimate relationship. The cautious commitment of living together results in two people, figuratively speaking, having one foot inside the door and the other outside, and then wondering why they feel so insecure with each other. If you have a fear of commitment and a subconscious belief that your partner is going to leave you anyway, that's usually what happens—they leave you! They find somebody else to take your place.

Let's examine a few of the possibilities. First of all, a woman in her psychological contract is subconsciously looking for a husband. For example, a woman wants a man who knows where he is going, who has goals, ambition, and drive. That means he will never be unemployed and that he will always take care of her financially. She may find someone who is hard-working, ambitious, and a goal-setter. She'll marry him and then complain that she married a work addict. She'll grumble that the man is compulsive in his work and can't think of anything but his preoccupation with his job. So many professional men are guilty of this fault. Women find that a man's preoccupation with his job and his books becomes a very difficult mistress to compete with. But that's what she asked for and looked for; and that is just what she found.

Going to the other extreme, a girl raised in a family with a father who was a hard-working business man, executive or a professional, who worked and worked, and never had time for his wife, time for fun or time for vacations says, "I never want to marry a man like that!" Her contract will be to search for someone who won't be driven the way her father was—who'll be fun, casual and take it easy—

who never thinks about tomorrow; who just relaxes and doesn't worry. She'll find him engaging and fun to be with, and yet she'll delude herself about his unpredictableness and wonder why she has to loan *him* money to take *her* out . . . . but that doesn't bother her because he's an easy going fellow, not a bit like her father.

She might marry him, only to discover that he *is* very easy going, irresponsible, and that he doesn't believe in hard work. He works, and if he doesn't like the job he either quits or gets fired. If he runs up bills and acts financially irresponsible, she's left with the dubious distinction of always answering the phone or trying to forestall or play games with one bill collector or another. And it's true, she selected the man who is just the opposite of her hard-driven, industrial giant, materialistic father. But she's not happy either.

Once in a while you may find a woman who has a need to mother a man or to rescue him. She'll see one with faults or character defects and say, "Well, he only needs someone who can love and understand him the way I can. I'll remold him and make a man of him. He just needs someone like me." So she'll marry him, only to realize that she can't re-make him. After so much effort and so many years, he is not clay in her hands but still just a very ineffective, immature, irresponsible man. Instead of her needing to be the one who rescues him, she now becomes the victim of her psychological contract.

In An Uptight World

The opposite extreme of this is the case of the woman who has been raised by a very dictatorial, authoritarian father. She has been tyrannized by him and made to feel that, no matter what she did, it was never right and she could never win his approval. Her psychological contract would be "Somebody please take care of me." Unfortunately, she may select someone just like her father; somebody strong and authoritarian, who will tell her what to do and what not to do and also when to do it. He will assume *all* of the responsibility. At first she'll say, "This is great!" But after fifteen years and six kids she wakes up one morning and thinks, "Hey, you know what? I've been doing quite a lot in this family, I really run this house. I make hundreds of decisions a week. I manage this home while my husband is earning a living and yet *he* feels that I don't have a brain in my head. He's the king and I'm a doormat." Then she gets depressed and may seek out a counselor or therapist to help her with the depression and thinks, "What a beast of a man I married!"

If the therapist isn't proficient he'll fall into the trap of saying, "You poor dear, you really ought to get rid of the fellow," without looking at *her* need to define her role in that relationship of "doormat of the year."

If it goes on long enough she may end up saying, "Look, Buster, I want more to say in this marriage. I'm not the weak person that you married."

And he'll say, "What's wrong? I thought you were happy. What's gotten into you now?"

To which she'll reply, "I'll tell you what's gotten into me. Here are the divorce papers. I'm leaving!"

And so, left with his divorce papers, the strong, authoritarian man is absolutely baffled and bewildered. From whence did the revolution originate? The trouble started when she wanted to become more of a person in her own right, not just a doormat.

I wish I could say that all human being were perfect; that they always knew what they were doing when they selected a spouse, but they don't. When talking with people married twenty and thirty years it's very interesting to discover most really don't know what they expected in a mate. When asked this the silence is deadly, and they stammer and stutter trying to find out exactly what they did expect in a husband or a wife. They had never thought about it! No wonder marriages have problems, and people are miserable. A young couple can be mature enough to take time before rushing into marriage to get to know each other very well, but then an unplanned event called pregnancy creates stress on their relationship. The wedding takes place, but unfortunately they were both left with questions that might haunt them the rest of their married lives. "Did she marry me because she was pregnant, or did she want to?" Or, "Did he marry me out of duty or out of love?" Until this mystery can be aired and discussed honestly it can be a ghost that haunts a marriage.

Occasionally a man will seek a very dependent-type woman. He has a need to be strong because he has doubts of his strength, and he looks for a woman who will be dependent upon him, thus allowing him to be the dominant one in the relationship. He will marry her, without realizing that she will be just what he sought; an irresponsible, poor housekeeper, and ineffective mother because she's an immature person. But—he won't admit that those characteristics led him to choose her. I wish I could say that men actually knew what they were doing when they got married. A woman, I believe, is much more intrigued with the art and selection of a man than a man is with the selection of a wife; although a man lives under the fantasy that he is the one who calls the shots. That's a nice myth to believe.

There has been a longing for us to be able to return to the 'good old days'. Unfortunately the return of the good old days is but a dream. For we live in a world where there is tension, increasing stress, and people have their own unique tolerance for their ability to handle problems. Anyone who has any awareness of what it is to be alive today, and to be married today, knows that there are many compounding pressures upon a marriage. I'd like to examine with you a few of the stresses of life and how to deal with some of them more effectively, so you can hang loose in your marriage and do a little more loving and less fighting. All right?

The biggest shock of all is that when we marry a person, so often the person we marry is really not the person we *thought* we married. After the ceremony and the honeymoon we take off our masks, quit our masquerade and games and say, "Surprise, surprise! This is who I really am!"

When the honeymoon is over we begin to discover that marital bliss does not just exist in the bedroom, but involves other rooms of the house. Then there is the routine of day-to-day living which is far less romantic than the courtship excitement of dating each week. We see stubby beards, hair rolled in curlers, clothes dropped on the floor, and we discover that neither in the first year of marriage is exactly a gourmet cook. We begin to perceive that marriage is not at all like it was in our youthful daydreams.

The first stress of married life is the attempt to deal with each others' differences and uniqueness. We get uptight and react negatively to the reality that another has the audacity to have a different idea, a different opinion, a different solution. It's strange that to be different is so easily labeled as bad, stupid or odd. How dare you be different! This is how the world is, forgetting that the only world of reality we know is our own. People are different, and we've all been programmed differently.

Before we were married we had no prior individual experience of our own, so when we are married, we subconsciously plug in the old computer—"How did mom and dad act when they were married?"

"How did they go about showing love and affection, anger and fighting."

"Who was in charge of the money."

"Who was in charge of the children?"

"Who planned vacations?"

Who did this and who did that. Each of us has that data bank there ready for us because we have observed it for a long time. In fact, the greatest sex education is that which a mother and father communicate to their children, verbally and nonverbally.

A mother tells her children what she feels and what she values in a man called the husband and father. He also contributes his feelings, evaluations, and criticisms toward the woman who is their mother. Sometimes the greatest gift that a father can give his children is to love their mother. Often times the word 'love' is confused with the need to be loved. One of the most frustrating surprises in marriage is to discover that each person has a half bucket of love and is hoping that the other will fill their bucket to capacity.

No matter how hard you try, you are always going to feel cheated if you are *waiting* to be loved, and haven't yet discovered the secret that love is like this: in order to keep it, you have to give it away. Instead of saying, "I need to be loved," you have to think of how well *you* are loving. How do you send the message to others that you love, value, and treasure them? Think about it! Do you reach out in love? If you do, you feel good about it. The wonderful part about it is that the person who reaches out and loves always ends up with far more than he ever gave away.

One of the most important areas of communication in marriage is the ability to listen and communicate. Each of us, far more than we're aware of, lives out our life programmed to outline who can say what, to whom, and at any given time. If we are different it doesn't mean that we must personalize and feel attacked because the other has said something contrary to what we believe, think or feel. We shouldn't feel that they are attacking us and disqualifying us as human beings.

Let's look at the aspect of exploring these differences without an altercation. There *is* more than one way to solve a problem. There may be many alternatives and solutions to the solving of your problems, and if you take the time to explore them you can hold off before exploding and going through the ceiling.

Many years ago I worked with a young couple in their late twenties. They had a very explosive relationship. There were the typical problems of never having enough money and the husband searching to find his role and identity in his job. They used to argue readily, accuse each other and counteraccuse.

I told them to sit down and search for ways to avoid an argument when they sensed trouble brewing. They both agreed to that idea. The husband was a very fiery fellow. One day they came in for a counseling appointment and the wife said, "Boy, did I blow it. I really blew it, Ken. Bob came home the other night and he was emotionally uptight, and I knew it. He said, 'Honey, I'd like to talk to you about your grocery money.' Well, that pushed my button and I went through the ceiling, screaming and hollering and playing 'uproar'. And he said, 'Hey, wait a minute. Come back to earth and sit down. We're going to explore the differences and not explode. I've come up with two possibilities: one, you're not controlling the money properly or, two, I'm not giving you enough money to manage the shopping.' I felt so foolish because I was ready for him to explode, and here he was so calm, not getting excited and willing to seek a solution to a problem in our relationship. We sat down and without attacking each other or accusing, looked at the data."

I asked her what she found out. Her husband turned to me and said, "Well, Ken, it's like this. I discovered that when we got all the facts on the table she had been managing the money very well. I just wasn't allowing her enough."

Oh, if we could ever think before we explode. We could explore all those differences and then we might be able to hang loose and not feel bitter and uptight so much. There's a popular myth that love is what makes marriage grow. When you ask, "What is Love?" you hear 57 varieties of the definition. Many believe love is a feeling. If love is just an emotion, then you're in trouble because sometimes you just don't feel very loving. You feel depressed. You feel frustrated, or angry, and you don't see any great stars bursting in the air and rockets going off, and so you say, "I guess I'm not in love anymore." You don't fall in love, I'll tell you that? Love, basically, as I see it, is the ability to give, and to listen to one another to try to understand who the other is. Then we may develop the quality of a relationship where each person has permission to be more open, more honest with each other without fear and without threat, and thus reach a depth of intimacy in that way. It's wonderful to discover, "Hey, we can communicate on a level that I have never before communicated with another human being." That kind of relationship would be defined as a *loving relationship*.

Oh, how hard it is to learn to listen, but love is listening. One time at a national dental convention I made the statement that professional men were often lousy lovers because of their preoccupation with their work. This quickly resulted in a great deal of hissing and booing. I thought they were going to run me out of town or hang me from the nearest tree. But before they did I asked them to look at the words I had written on the chalk board. "Love is Listening". "Please, gentlemen," I said, "before you jump to conclusions, would you allow me the privilege of asking your wives, your children and your staffs how they would rate you as a listener?"

Well, from an angry mob, ready to riot, there developed a quick silence because of the realization that they weren't good listeners. They could tell people what to do. They could decide for people. However, to really hear another person, not just their words but their feelings, their hopes and fears, they realized they were not good listeners.

What are some of the problems of listening? You were taught to read and write. Who in your experience has ever trained you in the art of listening? I'm sure that if you were honest you might rate yourselves as being a poor listener. The facility of listening begins to break down when you evaluate, judge, and criticize what the person is saying to you before you have completely heard the message. And if you hear something that is perhaps a little hostile, this causes you to become defensive. The minute *you become* defensive the quality of your listening ability diminishes. This is because you are thinking of how you can retaliate. When you drift off on daydreaming trips while someone is struggling to communicate with you, you look beyond them. You're not listening.

When I went to graduate school, many of my fellow classmates, as well as myself, were married and had children. A friend and I were talking of the hardships of going to school, working, and being a good husband and father. He said to me, "You know, the other night I was home reading and my little boy came in from playing and said to me, 'Daddy, Daddy,' I closed the book with my finger in it, marking my place, and all of a sudden he stopped and looked at me. He said, 'Daddy, are you going to take your finger out of that book and listen to me?'"

How often we put a finger in our book and don't listen. We're saying, 'Yes, yes, yes,' which only means to hurry up and get it over with and shut up! Once in a while you will hear someone who hears you without judgment, without criticism, and with empathy. You feel a warmth of acceptance and experience a sense of joy in this moment of time. You have had a real experience of humanness. You've encountered one another. When you really listen to another person you face the great possibility, that if you listen, you'll change.

We are bombarded by so many stimuli and perceptions, that in order to deal with them, our neurological system must label, interpret and store them so we won't be overwhelmed by them. In essence, when we receive a stimulus from our perceptual world we automatically interpret and label it. Our prior life experiences and emotional reactions to certain words are recorded as our own private meanings. This automatic and individualized process can hinder our ability to listen.

I will never forget the time when I was very much involved in working with teenagers and the drug culture. My oldest son was then fourteen, and he said to me, "Dad, since you started to specialize in working with teenagers you've become a better father".

I'm glad that he could trust our relationship to say that I was improving as a father. It's always nice to know that you can improve. When I began to examine what he meant, I realized that I spent most of my day listening to teenagers; wearing their odd costumes and weird glasses, complete with long hair and bare feet, and speaking the strange lingo of the drug culture. For this reason I was challenged to find the person behind the facade, behind the uniform, the gadgetry and the gimmicks. If I could wait long enough to *hear* them, I discovered that what I had previously labeled or interpreted had to change; and so did I. That's the trick of it all.

When I began to hear another person, I had to change what I thought, felt or interpreted about that person. Sometimes we resist change. Sometimes we prefer to label, stereotype and pigeonhole people rather than spend the energy to hear them in their uniqueness. As a psychologist I am so overwhelmed by human behavior that I realize that I can never begin to understand it completely because of the everchanging, evolving nature. For that reason I've not found psychological tests useful. I cannot find a therapeutic value in labels. They prevent me from knowing the person with whom I'm counseling. Labels are barriers for lazy and fearful people to hide behind.

The High Cost of Marriage

The high cost of being married today places an exceptional strain on many young couples. One of the variables that create the pressure may be an unconscious desire to begin the marriage somewhat in the style and comfort of their parents. They fail to appreciate the years that have passed which have made it possible for them to reach their present state of comfort and luxury. The cost of buying or renting a home, food, gasoline and taxes burden many young people who have been sheltered by their parents who have protected them from facing the economic facts of life. Money pressures are guaranteed to produce one thing—constant strain on the relationship—which brings out the worst in all of us.

I know we sometimes like to be idealistic and say that money isn't the issue, or it isn't important. But when you are faced with bill collectors, and you've lost your job due to some kind of phase-out, and there's nothing to fall back on—then, yes—money is very important! The wisdom of sound financial planning is very essential for a good marriage relationship. Economic pressures are one of the largest precipitating factors in drawing out all of the ugliness you would just as soon hide. This very often leads to the divorce court. The fact that they can't even afford the divorce is the next big jolt! Attorney's fees and two separate houses make the strain even greater financially making the couple feel trapped in a marriage that one or both parties no longer wants.

Another stress situation I'd like to deal with is that lethal hour of the day I call the "Arsenic Hour". This is the time of day just before the dinner hour. The husband has had a hard day at work, is hungry, with acid pumping in his stomach and adrenalin flowing from all the frustrations of his work. The traffic is heavy, and the tension builds. Meanwhile back at home his wife has been running around filling her many roles and duties from taxi driver to cub scout leader, to changing diapers and delivering cookies to the PTA meeting. She has chased children and tried to meet all their needs, and on top of that, she must start to prepare dinner. Now *she* has feelings of frustration as the kids whine and tug at her skirt, and she wonders if she can hold on until her husband gets home. The Arsenic Hour is not a sight to behold or look forward to each evening.

Finally father turns into the driveway and is met by screaming wife and children. Everyone is sending messages—"Please hear me!" "Please make me feel good!" "Please let me get rid of my frustrations." —messages that no one hears. Pretty soon the man says, "OK, everybody, get out of my way. I've had a rough day at the office."

He no sooner says that than Mom says, "What are you going to do about Pete?"

"For crying out loud, do I have to come home and

be the disciplinarian too? Can't you handle your children by yourself? I don't want to come home and have to punish Pete." And Pete breathes a sign of relief and thinks he can now run off to his room because his mom and dad will fight and soon forget about him. So Mom sulks in the kitchen and bangs a frying pan around, and Dad picks up the paper, and perhaps a drink, and tries to get his head together. Finally his wife comes back into the living room and finally says, "Dear . . . ," because he's been silent now and the kids are a little in awe and afraid of him, "you're not mad at me are you?"

"No, honey, just let me be".

She goes back into the kitchen and then comes back and says, "You're sure you're not mad?"

Then the little thought runs through his mind. 'No, I'm not so sure that I'm not mad at you. Just ask me one more time, baby, just one more time'.

She does and he just blows up.

"You bet your life I'm mad at you."

Then she says, "How dare you attack me. Here I am working all day for you, and I'm not having the fun of getting out and going to work, and meeting and talking with adults. I'm trapped with these kids and all of these 'duties'. You have it made in life."

"What do you mean, I have it made?" And the game starts!

The game is called "Uproar": the slamming of doors, the screaming, and the hollering. The night is ruined. The husband has a feeling that when he turns off the lights to go to bed that his wife won't be turned on.

It's stupid to not recognize the lethality of this hour before supper when physiologically, as well as psychologically, we're not equipped to deal with problem solving. The last thing many husbands need is one more problem to solve before dinner.

When Jeannie and I were first married and living in Minneapolis we had one of those stupid Arsenic Hour eruptions. I came into the apartment and on to the kitchen. Before you knew it we just exploded, and both of us went right through the ceiling. Like a lot of outbursts, I can't remember what it was about and neither can she. But that is not the issue . . . we exploded. I quickly thought to myself that it was rather stupid to have put so much emotion and anger into nothing. (I've always found that thinking helps!) I retraced my steps, leaving the apartment and closing the door. I waited a second or two and knocked on the door. She opened it and there she was, just as angry as ever. She looked at me and said, "Well?"

I swallowed hard and said, "Honey, we blew the first one so badly that I thought we should take two. How was your day?"

Well, that did it! She laughed and I laughed. There are times when we must be able to laugh at ourselves and our behavior. Each couple may have to find their own ways to live through these Arsenic Hours without becoming so uptight and blowing up into a game of Uproar.

We've worked things out quite well. I've learned to verbalize what I feel; what's going on inside of me. When she says, "Something bothering you?" as I am sitting there quietly, I don't say, "No, nothing," because something *is* bothering me. I've learned how to say what I'm feeling and not deny it. It's a reality to me. When I come home after ten hours or so of work and Jeannie says, "What's new?" I tell her it's been one of those days. My head is all messed up and would she please give me ten or fifteen minutes to get it together again. I ask her not to personalize my silence because it has nothing to do with our relationship. If I don't say that, she is likely to feel I'm angry with her. It's very important that she understands that I am not angry with her, but that I just need those few minutes to get myself together and forget my tiring day. She's learned to wait. It hasn't been easy, but she has learned to have patience until I can become more civil and human again without personalizing my silence. We've been able to live more peacefully without falling into the deadly trap of the Arsenic Hour.

Sometimes men need to understand the emotional state they're in and, instead of heading home right at that moment, just close their office door, take their shoes off, put their feet on their desk and listen to a little music until the worries and frustrations of the day pass. Call your wife and tell her you'll be a little late; that you're trying to get your head together. When you get into the car, watch your body. Are you grabbing the steering wheel like you want to break it in half? Is there tenseness in your jaws and forehead? Then stop a second and just relax your muscles. You can't fight the traffic or play leap frog. You just have to go along with it. Be alert and you'll get there by and by. You'll be in much better condition than if you went out and tried to fight it.

Another way of dealing with the Arsenic Hour is for the husband to say, "Honey, let me go take a shower, then I'll be more civil." Or he could say to the kids after giving them a hug, "Hey, I'll see you all later". Or you could just tell them that Mom and Dad need a few minutes together to just sit and talk and relax. Whatever you do, find *what works for you*. Break up the virulence of the Arsenic Hour.

You've heard dozens of jokes about the trouble in-laws can cause in a marriage. I must confess to you that when I married Jeannie I discovered she had two of the finest parents you could ever hope for, so I'm not a real expert on dealing with difficult in-laws. My in-laws have been very close to me and have been my friends all the years of our marriage. You might call me a little bit weird because I got my mother-in-law a mink stole before I got my own wife one. They have never once tried to tell us what to do, or how to do it. Those are words to live by and I hope I remember them when I am an in-law.

One of the first decisions to be made by a couple after they marry is that their new family unit comes first. If they haven't made that decision, there is an opening for real trouble. You shouldn't be made to feel guilty if you want to have a Christmas or other holiday dinner in your own home. Instead of always going to the home of parents or grandparents, invite them to your house. A new family should build their traditions and give themselves to the building of this family unit. Parents mean well when they offer advice or financial assistance, but often are not aware that with their advice or money comes a hooker called 'Let me win; let me control; let me have the final word.' Since many of us have been programmed not to speak back to our parents we easily feel guilty for accepting money and *not* accepting the advice or control. Guilt produces anger but few people can speak openly and honestly, or communicate to a parent that they don't want to have their guilt button pushed.

Abe Lincoln said so long ago, "Tell the truth and you won't have so much to remember." This doesn't mean that you should be cruel in your truth, but rather that you learn how to speak the truth in love. For instance, recently a woman told of the trouble she was having with her mother-in-law who was forever trying to protect her son, a man in his middle forties. She offered advice on cooking to "Let me take care of this," "Don't ask Fred to do that; it's too hard for him," or "I think if you bought this piece of furniture it would really fit the decor," etc.

Naturally the wife felt replaced and disqualified as a person. When the husband realized what effect this was having on his wife they decided to have a united front. Thereafter when his mother tried to manipulate and control their relationship, they found they didn't have to accept her maneuver for control or her attempt to make them feel guilty if they didn't follow her words. They could say, in essence, "Look, Mom, we promise never to tell you how to decorate your home if you promise never to try to tell us how to decorate *our* home. We appreciate your advice but we don't need it. We're grown people now. If you get upset about it because we said no, I guess that's your problem. We still love you but we will not accept your need to control and tell us what to do. We can do it ourselves." They're about to be grandparents themselves so they certainly are old enough. Of course the mobility of modern American society has solved many in-law problems. Three thousand miles helps a lot.

To help you break up the negative "Ain't Fair" tape in regard to in-laws, it is perhaps time for us to look at them as human beings, with faults and hangups just like the rest of us. If you see them with a problem and they are unable to deal fairly with you, or if they try to maneuver you through guilt in order to control, you don't have to hate them or feel guilty for not going along with their game. You can honestly say to yourselves, "That's their problem, not ours." It is their faults, their weaknesses, their humanness that you recognize, but you can remember that that's their problem so you can be prevented from feeling so used and abused and from being hooked by their failings. Remember, no one is perfect and that includes you and me.

Relationship Wars in Marriage

For about twenty years I have been listening to married couples describe their relationship wars between the 'nagger' and the 'naggee'. I don't think I have ever had a husband or wife ask me what they are doing that disturbs the other. Instead they complain about what the other person is doing to them. For example, in an interview a wife may say, "The real problem in our marriage is that my husband won't talk. He just locks himself up in his own little world and just grunts and says a few words. He just will not communicate with me."

Then the husband counterattacks with, "Just a minute, now. The reason I won't talk to you is because you are on to me all of the time, nagging about this and bitching all the time. That's why I withdraw into my own shell."

And they go on and on, with her still wanting him to listen and communicate with her beyond grunts, and to let her know that she's a person in her own right. And again he claims that if she wouldn't nag, he would talk to her more. You get the feeling that this relationship war could continue indefinitely, each person feeling justified since he is only reacting to the other. Both parties are blind to the responsibility of their own behavior in responding to the other, which determines the other's reaction.

To bring an endless relationship war to a close, I try to select the most reasonable one in the relationship and seek his or her cooperation in breaking it up. When asked to help end a war the first reaction is that I want them to give in to the other. I don't ask that; only for them to agree that this is hurting both of them. They readily agree that they don't want it and they hate it. Then I tell them that if they could change the nature of the outcome of this war, to de-escalate it, for instance, it would not be a sign of weakness, but a sign of strength. To contribute something to end a relationship war you could end up being lovers, and have an enjoyable time with each other. That doesn't mean weakness or capitulation. A person who can create a change in a relationship and give it solid ground to stand on is a strong person.

Let me give you an illustration. There was a very dynamic, successful, business man. He was authoritarian, dogmatic and rigid. One of the major complaints boiled down to this. He said his wife was cold to him; frigid, he guessed. His wife's reply was, "He comes home from work, we have dinner, and then he picks up the Wall Street Journal and hides behind it. He won't talk. But then when we go to bed he's ready for me to turn into an instant lover after he's ignored me all night."

When I heard the repetitiveness of this boring war

I asked the wife, because I thought she was more flexible, for an appointment alone. We agreed the way they were living out their lives was very painful and miserable. I asked her to just stick to one resolution for one evening. This was that she would not let anything stop her from being able to give the relationship something so that the outcome would be pleasurable, and not war. For instance, Friday night she would feed the children early. Before her husband came home, she would take her shower, slip into a beautiful gown and use her best perfume. Set the table for two with candlelight and wine and cook his favorite dish. She was to remember that she would not allow *anything* to stop her from breaking up this war. She said she would do it.

The next week when she came back I asked her how it went. She said, "Well, Ken, I did everything you said. Took a shower, had a lovely gown on, got the kids fed; had candlelight and wine and the kids were all away. He came home and was quite surprised that I was trying to be extra pleasant, and he did enjoy the meal."

I asked her what happened next.

"Well, when I was clearing off the table he went into the living room and sat down again, picked up his blankety—blank books and began to read."

I asked her what she did then.

She said she just stood there in the kitchen and fumed and fussed.

I said, "I know, you turned on the *Ain't Fair Blues* tape."

She answered in the affirmative.

I told her that she didn't finish the task; that she probably had him so bewildered that he was sitting there in all likelihood looking at the Wall Street Journal upside-down, wondering what was coming off and hoping he knew. But she quit; she didn't finish the task. She let one little bit of resistance stop her. Now the next time that she does it, if he goes into the living room and picks up his books and hides behind them, she should just walk over to him and put her arms around his neck and whisper in his ear, "Don't forget what all that candlelight and wine was all about." I defy *any* man with any sense at all not to break the silent war and begin to want to know what's coming next.

"Come to think of it, he was rather amorous that night and he was trying to show me exceptional tenderness."

I asked her what she did.

"I hit him!"

I asked her to handle it my way and she agreed to finish the task and not let anything stop her.

The outcome of this was wonderful. They laid down some ground rules for what they could talk about and their own needs for private times.

He was able to say things like, "Every time I want to talk to you, it's always one more problem with the children and I'm tired of hearing about that."

She could say, "Well, the thing that frustrates me about you is that every time you want to talk to me it's about a business venture, an investment or some complex economic problem, and I'm just not interested."

So they made a deal. For their private time they would eliminate children and business talk, and limit it to what's going on between them.

I know it's hard because you sometimes feel real injustice when the other hasn't been fair to you. We have a saying, "When there is something about me I don't want to see, I have a hard time looking at me." So you can raise the possibility that perhaps you are contributing far more to the relationship war than you want to admit to yourself. If that's so, do you want to make the decision that you want to give to the relationship, to end the war, and have more intimacy and fun in your marriage? I don't care what you do—anything that will help relieve the tension. My favorite gimmick was to put out a white handkerchief and wave it around the corner. Jeannie would say, "I'm not going to fall for that again. You can't get me to laugh this time." I'd keep on waving it and soon she'd start laughing, and the war would end. Find out in your own way what would work in your own relationship to prevent if from being so uptight.

Destructive Communications

One of the first things to stop so we can hang loose in our marriage is our destructive communications. Maybe I shouldn't give you some of these examples in the fear that you might practice them. But hopefully, if you want to learn how to hang loose, experience more love and have more fun in your marriage, you need to recognize a destructive communication and put an end to it.

One such example is the habit of always interrupting or changing the subject so that a statement or transaction can never be completed. The frustration of the incomplete transaction is felt when you are trying to have someone listen to you but the other person interrupts you before the message is complete; or changes the topic of conversation; or attacks you before he has heard you; or just walks away leaving you with a dangling participle. It is frustrating to know that nothing has been resolved; that nothing has been finished. You are left with psychic energy that has no place to go, and the problem has not been resolved. This can be turned into a negative tape with all of this inner-disappointment. The other person may be completely unaware of how stymied you are and how frustrating he is in the relationship.

Silence is a very tricky way of controlling a person. You can always come up with, "Sorry, but I didn't hear you." That means "I'm really not responsible."

Sometimes it's very obvious that the use of silence is punitive because it never allows the other person the right to get feedback and know where you stand in the relationship. You're left with your wild imagination to envision the worst and to fear the worst.

There is another aspect to the use of silence. The

person using silence to control the relationship also becomes trapped by his own silence. When he sends a message to another person and they reply with silence, usually the person who sent the message quits, and just suffers indignation and frustration at being controlled by the silent maneuver. But you don't have to quit just because someone responds in silence. I know that one wife recently told me that the way she got her husband's attention was to scream and throw things on the floor. There must be a better way than a tantrum to get another's attention.

If you want to break up the silence then stick with the initial transaction. Speak about the silence. "Do you know how frustrating your silence is to me. How long are you going to be silent? Do you think you can crawl away in a shell and withdraw from the world and not face the fact that we need to get something resolved, now, tonight, and not let it go over until tomorrow and contaminate tomorrow." Ask if there is something you've done that is bugging the other person. Tell them you'd rather have them speak up. Let them know that their silence is driving them up a wall.

Another destructive communication is the dishonest answer. The husband gets a message from his wife to do something, and he doesn't jump with great joy and enthusiasm in doing it. However, he realizes that maybe he had better do it whether he likes it or not! So, he says, "Honey, I'll do it now, I'm sorry I said no."

She replies, "No, it doesn't matter; it doesn't matter. I wouldn't want you to do it. I'll do it myself."

"But Honey, I'll do it."

"No, it wasn't important. It was nothing. Just go ahead and watch your ballgame. I'm sorry I broke into your world. I had no right to do that." Now she is beginning to pull the martyr game. "Poor me."

The husband says, "But I'll do it!"

"But dear, you didn't really want to do it."

"Well, no, I didn't want to do it. But I thought about it and said, yes, that's a reasonable request." Then later on he says, "Honey, is something wrong?"

"Oh, nothing's the matter; nothing at all."

That's dishonest. Sure, there's something the matter. You can ask something of another in a relationship; but by the same rule you don't have to demand that they emotionally jump up in ecstasy and turn cartwheels because you wanted one of your needs met.

Mind reading is another trouble spot. A person says, "I know what you're thinking, or feeling; and I'm mad at you for it."

Then you say, "That isn't what I was thinking."

"Yes you were. I know who you are. I know how you think and act. You really didn't want to do that."

How's a person to convince a mind reader that he has read your mind wrong. The mind reading ploy is also seen when one person tries to outguess the other. This person will think of a message he would like to send to you. But, being a mind reader, he thinks he knows how you will answer, and it won't be the correct answer. So he gets upset without realizing he has never sent the message to you. He has not only sent the message inside his own mind, but has answered as well. This is unfair and destructive communication.

A teaser is also a destructive communicator because if the one being teased responds, "That hurt. It wasn't funny at all," the teaser has a neat copout by saying, "But I was only kidding. Don't take yourself so seriously." It doesn't help the person being teased, because to be made fun of or put down by another still hurts.

How to Develop Some Good Communication Ground Rules
to Prevent Destructive Communication

Married couples need to solve difficulties without becoming destructive. First of all, watch the Arsenic Hour. That's no time to problem-solve for it will only end up with arguing, hurt feelings, and slamming of doors.

Discover in your own relationship what things the other person does that irritate you the most and then talk about them calmly and not accusingly. Let's learn to eliminate some of the communication 'fouls' such as dirty name calling. All it accomplishes is to hurt the other person. But you say it's getting hostility out. Hostility just for the sake of hurting is destructive.

Fouls are also caused when people are talking on a certain problem of the here and the now, and one of the parties starts bringing in the old problems and memories of yesterday, or some dig about the relatives of the other person. Soon you not only have the problem of the here and the now, but five, ten or twenty years of problems dumped on the table before you. It's no wonder that you get overwhelmed and defeated.

This ground rule might be to just keep the discussion with what's going on here, right at this moment.

Look at your sense of timing. Is it right? In other words, it's not fair to dump big problems on your husband just as he is walking out the door for work. He knows he has to leave and resents problems dumped on him when there is not time to deal with them. He gets into the car and becomes a highly accident-prone individual due to the frustration and anger he's feeling inside. He knows that was a dirty foul. It couldn't solve anything and all it did was make him miserable.

Another good idea to remember is not to solve anything when one person or the other has consumed too much alcohol. Don't waste time on drunk talk. Don't use alcohol as an excuse and say, "But this is the only way I can get it off my chest." Then, after you have devastated someone, don't say, "Well, it's not my fault. I had too much to drink."

It's also time that couples begin to take a look at

the use of and abuse of chemical pills and alcohol in their relationship. If that's the only time you can say what you think you need to say, then you're looking for a problem. It's a neat copout to say you just weren't yourself so you should be forgiven.

There's much violence that comes out when drunk talk is going on. The police will tell you that the most dangerous call they make is when they answer a request for assistance in a family fight. A policeman is most likely to get injured trying to break up a fight, and if the people have been fighting with alcohol as a fuel it can become a very destructive and violent thing. So if someone has had too much to drink, make it a rule never to listen. Just leave and go someplace else.

It's time for you to stop and look at yourselves. Learn how to listen to yourself. Ask what is really upsetting you. Was it something that happened earlier in the day. Was it a negative tape you were playing? Is all this arguing and fussing just nitpicking? Is it something basic that you're not talking about? Is there something you'd like to say but somehow feel that you can't?

If you want to be honest why don't you begin by asking what you're doing that is hurting the other person. How are you frustrating the other's needs? Very often as we begin to examine ourself, we find that we are our own worst enemy. Life is too short to be uptight and bitter, carrying around a load of anger that's ready to explode at any moment of time.

This is what's wrong with the strong, silent type. His stoic behavior says 'peace at any price', but then one incident, one event, will finally get to him and then he will explode like a volcano and erupt all over the place. Learn how to deal with your frustrations, your emotions. Open up honestly about what's bugging you. Look for the feedback in a relationship to correct mistakes. Very often you'll discover that what you thought the other person was upset about with you is not the truth at all. You have been angry for all of the wrong reasons.

There's no way I could write a chapter concerning marriage without also spending a few words about sex. I'm not going to devote too much time on this subject as there have been so many books and articles written recently about the subject. I would like to talk very briefly about sex as a joy or a weapon in marriage. I have a feeling that we have become more open and aware; that we're not only talking about sex behind closed doors or in locker rooms, but have become much more reasonable and sensible and much less fearful of discussing the subject openly and honestly. One of my concerns is that we reduce sex to a matter of mere mechanics where the passions, the feelings and emotions are gone. Maybe we need to realize again that a woman is a far more complex person, emotionally, psychologically, and spiritually in what she thinks and feels about sex than is a man. A man who is known for his sexual exploits is given a favorable commendation. He's called a stud, or a real man. Whereas a woman, if she's known for her sexual exploits and extra-curricular activities is defined in derogatory terms as a whore or some other dirty name.

Sex in marriage plays a very different role than when it is viewed as a series of brief encounters between two people. Sexual intimacy is knowing the other and giving to the other. We have come a long way in our understanding of woman. We are no longer programmed to believe in sex as just a duty a woman must perform for a man for the conceiving of children. The feeling that a woman has of intimacy and the need of someone who is tender, who's a communicator and a listener, is very important to her.

The joy of sex for a woman doesn't begin in the bedroom and this is hard for men to understand. A woman looks for little things, the sensitive things, that let her know in a thousand ways, "I'm thinking of you, I care about you, I value you."

Also I believe a woman needs to be able to say the same things to her husband. Don't assume that he doesn't need to hear from you, "You're neat. I'm glad you're out there working hard for us. I sometimes take for granted the hours you put in for our family; I know there are times you'd like to be home relaxing instead of working. Thanks for being such a fine person."

When sex is used as a problem-solver, there is a new problem. A man would like to solve the interpersonal problems through sexual relations with his wife. The majority of women would rather say, "Let's resolve the problems and the tensions, and then I'll be free of bitterness and resentments and be able to enjoy the intimacy of our relationship."

I'm not saying either is right, or wrong. I don't feel that sex should be used as a weapon to bargain with to win your case, or to withhold sex as a punishment. If you do that then you should not be surprised when sex is turned against you. In a world full of stress and pressure you may even have to fight for more time for intimacy. You may even have to plan instead of just to let it happen, so you can maximize your time together in order to enjoy more fully all the warmth, softness, and the joy of finding each other again. If we don't work at it, plan for it and strive for it, all too often as the years roll by we become dulled and trapped. Boredom and routines turn into ruts, and this is the outcome. Someone made a pun and said that love that is taken for granted turns into granite. Old marriages don't die, they just fade away.

It's very interesting to ask a couple what they do for fun; how they enjoy each other. I don't mean just get lost in a crowd at a party . . . what they do that's fun.

Marriage is never the same; it's always in a state of change and flux due to pressures, growth, different kinds of problems that must be solved and resolved and adjustments made. About the only thing we can say about a marital relationship is that it is always under constant change and pressure. The first change is getting to know who the other is and who "I" am in relationship to "You."

The next real big change comes along when the first child is born. This can be the most critical time in a marriage; a time of crisis. The husband may resent the fact that his wife is now all wrapped up in the role and the energy of being a mother. He may feel left out and may spend more and more of his time working and seeking other activities. It's easy for the man to fall into the trap of putting all his energies into his career, and the wife putting all of hers into being a good mother to the new baby.

Families are always going through changes. As there is only one first child, there is only one second child. How soon did the second child come along? Was it planned for? How did they feel about it? How many more demands are placed upon the mother and the father? The family changes even more when the first child enters school. We find ourselves involved in more routines, and yet may have more free time, if we give ourselves permission to enjoy our free time.

Pressures of Marrying Too Young

Teenage marriages show a very high mortality rate. Psychologically they're still going through a period of self-growth and development. They may have gone through their first adolescent rebellion and now they are going through the second stage of psychological integration. They need to find out who they are; what they want to retain of their parents' values; what they would like to preserve of their peers' values; and also to examine what they have personally experienced.

Two people may be very close at age sixteen, having a common interest in horses, rock groups, etc. But that is not enough. From sixteen to twenty-two young people are psychologically maturing, and, through psychological reintegration, the two people can become very different people at twenty-two than they were at sixteen.

Thus a young girl who marries perhaps to escape home, because of pregnancy, or because all the other senior girls are doing it, may later act out what I call the Twenty-eight-year-old Syndrome. Now don't ask me why I picked twenty-eight. It just seemed for awhile that I had several women come to me for counseling who were this age. They did have several factors in common. They were married right after high school; their motivation was to leave home or they were pregnant. But they didn't mind that—they were glad to be on their own and were excited to have the romanticism of setting up their own place. But now they're twenty-eight, with two or three kids; their husbands were working hard. All of a sudden they felt a gnawing restlessness and envy of girls who were single and eighteen. Wistfully they would like to be that age again, only this time they wouldn't have jumped into marriage. They longed for the joy of living their own life without the responsibilities of a husband and children, and a house to clean. They resented those lost years of freedom. They met a friend at a bridge party, or had a neighbor who also felt trapped and the two of them would get together and compare their "ain't fair" tapes and would feel very sorry for themselves. After all, it's the vogue to want to be a liberated woman today. So the two young women began to pal around together and would go out to bars and other places. They found that other men were noticing them and flirting with them. The attention was exciting. It reassured them of their sexual attractiveness because they were getting close to thirty years old and somehow had the weird idea that something terrible was going to happen then.

Well, believe me, nothing awful happens at thirty except that another day passes. The husband can be completely baffled as to what his wife is so upset about, to what she is demanding. Before he can catch his breath, she may be demanding a divorce. If they don't get professional help at that time and try to understand the psychological dynamics, they may make a very foolish mistake and dissolve a marriage which could be saved.

Another strain found in marriage as it goes through its process of evolution and change is the mobility of people. We lived in the San Fernando

Valley in Southern California for nine years. New subdivisions were built, and before they were finished their first occupants were putting up "For Sale" signs in the front yards. In fact, I had the impression they were moving and selling their homes faster than they were selling their cars. This constant moving creates a strain on the marriage. With this strain is the feeling of a lack of commitment and no sense of belonging to a community. This puts a responsibility on the family unit to satisfy its emotional needs. Often the family cannot meet that stress and pressure.

Without a doubt, one of the next periods of crisis is the discovery that there is now a teenager in the family. Unfortunately, to be a teenager is often synonymous with being a "juvenile delinquent". I'll devote much of the next chapter on ways to survive this period of their life. Seriously, I hope it will help you understand the teenage years better so you as parents won't be so uptight when the time comes.

The Middle Years

It's common knowledge that the woman's middle years are often filled with problems, but they can be extremely strenuous for the man also. During this period of his life he can become very introspective, and if he has not reached the goals or aspirations he set for himself as a young man, it can be difficult to accept. He looks in the mirror and sees he's a little paunchy and balding. Also he's had enough disappointments to dull his enthusiasm for life. He realizes he doesn't have too many years left to make his mark in life. Perhaps he senses he's been too involved in business and realizes he has paid too high a price for a life of work, work, work. Where did all the years go? How fast his children have grown and he wonders if he really knows them.

For the woman the middle years, the menopause, have been a specter haunting them. At least women have been forewarned and medically aware as to what actions to take, but who helps the man prepare? There are some good news however. Since the increase in longevity, middle age begins in the fifties instead of the forties.

It could be because I'm in my forties, or as a result of twenty years of counseling and listening to women, I feel that they have been made to feel guilty and uneasy about their self-worth for many reasons. I'm not writing as a "Woman's Libber" (whatever that means), but as one who feels the need to speak out against some of the psychological abuses to which women are and have been subjected.

There have been many books and articles written on the art of being a good parent or mother; that in the deluge of new theories and strategies women are swamped to the point that at times no matter what they do they have a twinge of guilt and doubt. "Is this the right way?"

For years numerous and unproductive studies

were conducted on what trait in a mother produces bad effect in her children. Completely ignored were husbands and fathers and their effect on the children and the family system. Also ignored was the effect that a child has on a parent, especially if that child is hyper-active or mentally retarded. Countless messages from the media make women feel like they are second-class citizens. She is just a housewife and mother. The impact is that she, as just a housewife or mother, really doesn't contribute much to society.

Then Madison Avenue helps our country glorify the "youth cult". Fashions, travel, the beautiful people concepts are geared to the worship of the youth cult. This intensifies the subtle disqualification that *when* you get older, it's all over except waiting to enter some fancy retirement community.

I think the middle years can be great! Personally, I feel there is a definite attractiveness that comes to women who have taken care of their physical health and later on they have a depth and charm that is very appealing. True, a woman who has spent a great deal of emotional and psychological energy in being a good mother will need to readjust her priorities. The children are about grown and she no longer needs to be "super mom", right on the job at all times. This is a critical time for her to reexamine herself; to grow and to rediscover the partnership called a marriage.

For those with marital problems one of the most revealing barometers of the middle years is disclosed by the comment from a husband who said, "We had a nice dinner together but discovered that when we finished talking about the children and my work, we had nothing personal to say to each other."

The special pressures at this time also are different. Couples who have stayed together for the sake of the children (which may not be doing them a real favor) may decide to end the marriage. What a waste of years waiting for *rigor mortis* to set in! There are alarming statistics reporting that one of the greatest areas of increase in divorce has been after the children are gone; people married twenty to thirty years. One person has outgrown the other. As he looks ahead to the next twenty-five to thirty years he honestly asks, "Do I want to spend it with this person, going through life in this old routine?" "Do we have the energy or capacity to discover again a new freshness to our relationship?"

I'll tell you one thing. These years can also be the most exciting, the most wonderful years. You should start to add up the plus values: that you might be reaching your economic peak; that the pressures of raising young children are behind you; and now you have more ability to do things as a couple, to travel, and enjoy a sense of freedom you haven't experienced for many years. The middle years do not have to be a devastating period of your marriage. They can be the most exhilarating, intimate years that you have. But, always be aware that the unfinished business of yesterday must be resolved so that the next thirty years can truly be creative, productive, intimate, joyous years.

An interesting point is that I have been delving into marriage as if everyone was married for the first time. With the number of divorces in our country we know that divorced people do remarry, and this does create a new set of problems.

For instance, how do you integrate a new family when one or the other partner brings children into the relationship? How do you allow the new husband and new father, or the new wife and mother, to develop a new family unit? The children are wondering who can say what to whom. "I don't have to listen to him; he's not my father," or, "She is only my stepmother." The one who has custody of the children often feels trapped between choosing between them and the new marital partner. Any time there is this kind of change, an attempt to rebuild a whole new family structure, I think it would be well for the couple and the family to seek a family counselor. They need to talk openly and honestly about their feelings; about what kind of a family, what kind of ground rules to have, and how long before they will be unafraid to trust one another.

One of the hardest roles to play in our society today is that of the divorcee. I have often been puzzled. Since there are two people who get the divorce —a man and a woman—where do the men go? Many women are without ways of meeting men. They become bitter because they don't like to go to bars. They think all the bars are full of men who want to hustle them and take them either to his place or theirs. It's hard for the single woman to be able to meet a man and not be paranoid about his intentions. The most difficult thing she will have to watch is that she does not allow herself the destructiveness of bitterness and self-pity. I don't have the answers for these problems but, I do wish there could be more understanding so a woman who is divorced or widowed will not feel that she is branded as a person of less worth.

If you are to continue to grow you must face the fact that you will have more time to count on yourself and your own ability, and to adapt and develop new resources and interests. If you don't, you can become very hollow and empty as you grow older. If you haven't learned how to cope with leisure time without trying to kill it, boredom can drive you to frustration and drinking too much. The sad fact is that you and I as human beings use only ten percent of our mental capacities. There is no reason not to find ways to live and enjoy life even in our final season. The latter years can be very rich if you keep your mind alive and curious.

I'll never forget one man whom I greatly admired. He was eighty-five years old at the time, and had had several heart attacks, but he had maintained a spirit of life. His eyes had a twinkle of excitement as he awaited the sunrise of the next day. He was always busy puttering around the house, working and fixing things; but most of all he had a talent for the earth, for the plants and flowers. One day I had received a call that John had had another heart attack. I went over to his house to see how he was. I knocked on his front door and waited. No one answered. I called without getting any response. Somehow I had a sneaky suspicion that John was not in the hospital, but in his own backyard. I went around the side of the house and there he was, slowly and lovingly working in his vegetable garden. I said, "John, I hear you had another problem with your heart?"

He replied, "Aw, I did, but it's all right."

"Shouldn't you be resting or taking it easy?"

"No. If I die and when I die, I want to be able to be doing what I enjoy and have a pocket full of seeds in my pocket, so when I go to Heaven I can go on planting and helping things to grow."

For him life was always a moment to be shared, and never to be dulled by boredom. He could find joy as long as he lived. The real tragedy is that I have known many teenagers at age fifteen who are emotionally and mentally dead. They intended to spend the next sixty years waiting for *rigor mortis* to set in because they thought life was boring and didn't realize *life* was not boring, but they were!

7

These People
We Call Our Sons
and Daughters

LISTEN TO THE CHILDREN
by
Kenneth J. Olson

Listen to the children as they laugh and play
and dream of floating on a cloud all day.
Listen to the children as they talk to a flower.
Why do you smell so sweet? How do you grow?
Where do you get your power?
Hey, Mister Wind, I can't see you, but the leaves
on the tree tell me you're making a breeze.
Where do you go, Mr. Wind, when the leaves on the
tree are again at ease?
Do you just go up in the sky so high?
Listen to the children explore their world
With searching eyes and asking a thousand "why's".

The Art Of Hanging Loose

See the children when they look at the parents
  in awe. You are so big and tall.
You don't have to prove you are good and wise.
This we already believe and can easily see with our eyes.
Just love us, that's all.

Listen to the children when they want to say,
  Please Mom and Dad don't shout and fight.
This makes us so afraid and uptight.
  Please someone say, "I'm sorry." Hug each other
real tight.
Then we'll know our world is safe for another night.

Listen to the children when they cry.
See their tears well up in their eyes and run
  down their cheeks like warm drops of rain.
They are learning the pain of not being heard today
Of hurting deep inside because no one thinks they're OK.

Listen to the children when one of them will say
  I just love my teddy bear cause he's soft and
  always the same each day.
He has bright button eyes and a sweet smile.
He's so real at times I forget he's stuffed with hay.
I love my teddy bear cause he never makes demands on
  me or tells me I've been bad.
He never makes me feel sad.

Listen to the children when one will crawl up on
  their grandpa's knee
Though your hair is silver and your hands shake,
  Your eyes are still bright and true.
I love you and you love me.
We both know what it's like to be put aside
But the stories you've told and the secrets we've shared

In An Uptight World

Fill me with a special pride.
I know you're old and some day you'll die.
I will cry and cry and pray that you didn't have to die.
But I'll always remember you and keep alive
The memories of the ways you showed me you cared.

Listen to the children when they go to bed at night
They wait for the footsteps and someone to hug them
real tight and say
I love you for being just you.
I'm so thankful I have you.
The warmth of the touch and the tenderness of the voice
wipe away all the tears and hurts from the day.
Enveloped with love all the fears of the night disappear.

Listen to the children when they pray
Thank you God for this beautiful day.
For the miracle I saw—a caterpillar becoming a
butterfly.
Thank you God for my home and all the good food
and a bed so soft
But most of all Mom and Dad who care.
Dear God I saw some people today with such frowns.
Help them to laugh again.
Send them a clown.
Open their eyes to see the beauty in the world.
All they could do was stare.
Help those people to listen to the music of your
beautiful world.
Thank you God for sending a baby to teach the
world about love.
Listen to the children when they pray
Love, love, love, that's what we all need each day.

This will not be a long dissertation on how to

raise your children as to what to do and what not to do, so don't expect a course in human growth and development. I would like to share with you some of the observations I have made of children, teenagers and parents through my years of counseling. It's not easy being a parent. Today there are more pressures, worries, and concerns than ever before in our times. We are not prepared to face a world with all of its complexities and stress. The rebellion of youth with the accompanying growth of the drug culture has frightened and immobilized us as parents too often.

One of the more basic decisions that we need to make about being parents is whether we want our children to love us or fear us. This means that both parents must make the decision. I'm of the old-fashioned opinion that I think fathers have a real opportunity and joy in being part of raising, nurturing, loving and caring for their children. Why should women have all the fun and all the work? A searching question, isn't it! Do we want our children to love us or fear us?

Let's take a look at what the results are when consciously or unconsciously you want your children to fear you. They must respect you; do what you say. In other words, if you are going to be a dictator and tell them how they shall live, think, and feel, dress, and what their goals shall be, you'll be trying to control much of their lives. And if a child lives with this fear of disapproval, displeasure and punishment, he naturally is living a very emotionally uptight existence for fear of making a mistake. The fear of never being all right with himself means that he never experiences the wonderful feeling of being accepted by the significant people in his life, his parents, and just being loved for himself.

You may argue and say you are not training your children in fear but to respect authority. If you hold back in giving them praise, or if you qualify that praise as if to communicate that they did a good job but that they should try harder the next time, the child feels that there is one more deed he must do, one more test he must pass, one more condition he must meet. This can cause him to become a very compulsively driven person. He never quite understands this because he thinks he is doing all right. He's obeying his parents, even if he is forty-five. Emotionally, he's still looking over his shoulder and saying, "Hey, did I do good enough now, Mom and Dad? Now am I good enough?" The sad part of it is that even when you search one goal after another, the acceptance still isn't there. So you tell yourself you'll just have to try harder the next time.

Emotionally, he who lives with this kind of fear is a very frustrated person. He's this way because he never came to terms with making peace with himself. He has haunting self-doubts that he can't trust his own thinking or his own feelings. He feels that his self-worth is never quite good enough, only if others say he is, then he might believe it. The person who is brought up under fear is trapped in the realization that the authoritarian person takes the responsibility for his behavior, and yet at the same time demands that he be responsible.

The parent who is the authoritarian places the child in a bind by saying, "I want you to be responsible." Still, the parent makes all the decisions, tells the child what to do, is the one who keeps the responsibility for himself and demands that the child perform in a praiseworthy manner. This does not allow the child to become self-sufficient. It is the means by which Hitler came into power. The German people had been so tired of the hard times and depression that they made a deal. "You be our dictator and we'll give you our freedom and our responsibility for our behavior." And this he did! At the end of the war, no one was guilty; they did just what they were told. "I'm not personally responsible; I just followed orders."

This is why the end result of a person raised in this atmosphere will be of passive acquiescence to life, or passive aggressiveness to people in authority.

In contrast, let's take a look at what it would mean if we raised our children with the idea that we want them to love us, not fear us. The word love is a rather sticky word in our language. We have so many various meanings to it. Sometimes when we say, "I love you," it means we have an angle, or it means blackmail.

If I were to give you a simple course of a few basic

things to follow in raising children, I would tell you this: If you want your child to grow up to love himself, trust himself, to love you and trust you and believe in you, you must communicate the same feelings to him. I bathed and put each of our children to bed every night, and I'd say, "You know, I love you for being just you. I'm the luckiest daddy in all the world to have such a sweet child as you."

This kind of love and a hug before you put them to sleep at night is never tied to any conditions or qualifiers. "I love you not because of your report card, or your talent, or because you're going to do a good job, but simply because you're you." The nicest thing about it is that they hug you back and tell you you're pretty nice, too, and they love you. That sounds very simple, doesn't it? But I tell you, it beats all the screaming and demanding that they obey, fear, and respect you. They go to sleep with that warm, wonderful feeling, "Gosh, they really love me for just being me."

Please don't make the mistake and say, "Oh, that means that you give them everything they want." No, that's not loving them. It's spoiling them, and giving them a false delusion that the world is their cupcake. It isn't. It doesn't mean that you can never say "No" to your child, but if you really love a child you can say no and not feel guilty about it. It might be better to display your love by not giving them so many advantages, but more of you. Also, if you want your children to love you learn to respect his need for privacy and daydreaming. Don't communicate to the child that he must always be a performing monkey. Each child is different, so you love them in their uniqueness.

My oldest boy started running at nine months. Mike didn't walk, he ran. Any parent who has a child born with a neurological rate of activity that is just a little higher than his own knows what it is to have a hyper-energetic, active child. He was a super athlete and could do so many things. For awhile my love of athletics was getting in the way of his growing up. I was too busy having him be an extension of me. I finally had to back off and let him just be himself. If he was going to love sports it would be because *he* loved them, not me.

My second boy was just the opposite. He was quiet and didn't particularly want to go outside and play. You'd see Danny sitting in his room when he was a little guy and you'd say, "What are you doing?" And he'd say, "Thinking." It's pretty hard for a parent to get upset with a child for thinking. But he was a thinker and he still is.

Mike had a devil-may-care attitude about everything, whether diving off a board at two-years-old, knowing that someone would be there to catch him, or dashing into a big wave at the ocean and come up spitting out sand and seaweed. Danny, on the other hand, could be placed on a towel at the beach and wouldn't think of putting his feet in the sand because he didn't like the feel of it.

Jeannie once asked me if Danny was a little different, and I told her, "Yes, he is different. Just keep on hugging him and let him develop at his own rate." Well, this quiet little boy who wouldn't put his feet in the sand went to Nicaragua, Central America, soon after he turned sixteen and spent three weeks there working as a paramedic. We asked Mike, who was then twenty, if he wanted to go with Danny and he replied, "Heck no, you wouldn't catch me doing anything that reckless."

What I'm saying is simply this. If you would surround a child with the security of love and communicate to him the feeling that you trust him to be himself and to develop at his own pace and uniqueness, then we have a wonderful surprise in store for us. Our little girl turned out to be a combination of her two brothers, a wonderful athlete and super student. She's a great little cook and has already spoiled her brothers with her "goodies".

The simple point is to realize that each person, even from their neurological rate of activity, is a unique individual and not an extension of ourself. They are not little adults. They are just children and you should allow them the privilege of being four without wishing they were six, and you can enjoy them at six without wishing they were eight or ten. Do you really want your children to love you? Number one rule—don't lecture. Spend ninety percent of your time listening. A child knows when you hear him. He'll tell you things because he knows he can trust you and your relationship. He can tell you about anything, and you'll hear him and give him understanding. He knows you'll help him find the answers and that you love him and then he knows he's for real.

Being able to have your child grow up and respect you sometimes means that you will have to take a firm, but reasonable, position with him. One of the key things is learning how to be reasonable. Learning how to have a child involved in making decisions with you is important in teaching personal responsibility. Give him an alternate of choice, even to the selection of what dress or shirt to wear on a particular day. Whatever it is about, the more you can ask him to participate in decision making with you, the more responsibility he will accept for his behavior.

That might backfire once in a while on you. I remember the mother who told me, "Thanks a lot, Ken. You told me about this alternate of choice. Well, my five-year-old turned it around on me the other day. We have a rule in our house that she cannot go outside after dinner. So the other night after eating, she came to me and said, 'Mother, can I go out and play in the front yard or the back yard?'"

Well, the truth is that children are very clever. I've also said that a child psychologist is a kid who understands his parents. It helps a child to own up to his own mistakes if a parent apologizes to the child for the errors he himself makes, and then asks for the child's forgiveness. I know that I have always done that and have discovered that the children are far more forgiving of me than I am of them.

A good term to use in negotiating decision-making within families is the word "reasonable", and that's a two-way word, by the way. It means that parents have to be reasonable as well as their children.

For example, when my oldest boy was fifteen-and-a-half he wanted to go on a double date. I think he was tired of his dad picking up his date, driving them to the game and then picking them up afterwards. That isn't the most thrilling thing. So he came to me and asked if he could go on this double date (he couldn't drive yet). I asked him where they were going, and he said to the game and to the dance afterwards. Then they wanted to go down the street to the pizza parlor. I asked him what time *would he like* to come home instead of telling him. He stammered around and said, "Twelve o'clock?" I agreed to that.

Next week the same request, same activity, but this time when I asked him what time he wanted to come home I said, "Mike, last week I asked you what would be a good time, and you said twelve and you were home by twelve. But that wasn't a reasonable decision."

He wanted to know what was wrong with it.

I thought for a moment and replied, "First of all I know that the dance isn't over until 11:30. I know the pizza parlor is just down the street, but after all, you aren't the only ones being served. Then your friend will have to take your date home and then get you home by midnight. That's not reasonable. He'd be breaking the law to do that. Now what time would you like to come home this weekend."

He looked at me, rather baffled, and said, "12:30?"

"Good, Your mom and I can sleep a lot better now because that's a more reasonable time."

Some of you might think, 'What if he had said 4:30 in the morning.' That's easy. That is not reasonable! No fifteen-year-old has any business out when it's against the curfew law. So you just state it to him. And don't back down. Don't buy the baloney that 'everyone else is doing it' because they're not. That's a con game, but if you have love and trust you can negotiate with each other.

What Does It Mean to Belong to a Family

We have a philosophy that we belong to each other as a family, and as such we do things for each other. That doesn't mean we are paid every time we pick up a dirty sock or dry a dish. If that were so the richest one in the family would be the wife and the mother of the kids. We just don't have (and by the way, this is no rule of judgment) allowances *per se*. We do feel that when there is an extra job to be done and extra time spent on it, we pay the children for it. And we do expect, as part of the family, that they keep their rooms picked up. We're not afraid to ask them for help. They all know what particular little jobs belong to them and very seldom is there any hassle. I feel that there is a much happier atmosphere when you begin to believe 'we really love each other'. It's a great feeling for the children too. It's neat to have grown teenagers who can still hug us and each other. That's their way of letting us know it's all right.

Wouldn't it be nice if rearing children was as easy as I've made it appear? But it's not. They're growing up and we're trying to live with their growing up and we find all different kinds of struggle going on. Our needs to have them do certain things are always interfering with their needs to do other things at the same time.

I also feel that any mother who successfully rears small children without going bananas deserves a medal. It's hard work and demanding work so I'm not going to give you a "how to" with simple steps to follow. Anyway, let's just take a look at a few of the struggles that I have noticed parents and children getting themselves trapped into.

Let's talk about school. This is a whole new world for the child. We may not think of him as being responsible, but at a very young age he has to learn how to get along with all kinds of children, teachers and their moods, and be able to have the autonomy of new learning experiences. He must learn how to compete and how to play games with people.

Sometimes he runs into a real character for a teacher. I'm not saying this happens too often but there is a real need for the parent to listen to what his child is saying. If they are having a particular problem with a school or a teacher, don't automatically jump to the defense of the adult. Do some more listening and investigating to find out just what does seem to be the problem. *Then* go down and find out where the problem lies. We often discover that maybe the problem *is* the teacher and a change should be made.

I know when it comes to parent teacher conferences for my children the teachers must have been thrilled to know a clinical psychologist was coming in for a conference. I felt it was very important for me to know what was happening and what type of person was working with my child. The schools have our children for a goodly number of hours, days, months and years. Their teachers have a very powerful influence over them, either to help them become winners or losers; to believe in themselves or not to believe in themselves; to be bored or to be turned on to life.

Schools place a great deal of pressure on children and I think we found an accelerated pressure when Sputnik first was launched. All of a sudden educators felt that our children should all become mathematicians and space engineers. Many of them did and are now among the unemployed.

In An Uptight World

One of the best things to communicate to your children is that you are going to encourage them to do their work, but basically it's going to be between their teachers and themselves. If a parent tries to get involved in his own needs to have a genius, or to have this done right, we often find a real power struggle and a destructive beginning.

During a counseling session with a teenager and his family the parents complained because their brilliant son was flunking. They said they didn't know what to do with him. They had tried this discipline, and that discipline, everything. They had nagged and tried to get him tutors and had gotten so involved in his education that they contaminated his desire to learn.

Finally the boy said, "Look, Doc, they can take away my driver's license, the car, my allowance. They can do all these things, but I can still flunk."

Words to live by—don't get involved with homework nagging. If a child is going to be responsible in handling his life, let him deal with the teacher about whether he got his homework done or not. If you get involved with him too often you start that old war with a nagger and a naggee. A parent nags and the kid says, "Well, it's their fault, not mine." And if things don't go right then he can say, "If they would just get off my back!"

Some parents have been so stupid that I have known them to say, "You shall study two hours a night, seven nights a week, or else." Well, they blocked out the two hours every night whether he had homework or not. And guess what? No homework was done. Resentment was there and bitterness was there, and the youngster learned how to kill time.

Relationship wars are dumb. I never will forget one we had in our home. When my oldest boy was fourteen he and Jeannie got into a real power struggle. They played the game. She would nag him about brushing his teeth, combing his hair, washing his face; not to forget his book, lunch money, bus ticket, and so on.

And he would say, "Yah, yah."

Then she would say, "You didn't brush your teeth," and he'd go back to the bathroom and turn on the water and she would go in there dutifully and feel the toothbrush. This continued until the two angry people muttered their goodbyes.

Well, I'm a country boy and was used to being an early riser and I loved the mornings. My wife at that time had nothing against mornings except that they came at the wrong time of day. So, I made a decision which would give me a peaceful morning and break up the war. I told Jeannie to stay in bed and not say a word to Mike about what he should remember or *anything*. All she could say was "Have a good day" as he was going out the door.

She said, "What if he forgets his books or his lunch money?"

And I replied, "Well then, he'll start to remember."

You know, he kept waiting for the nag and it didn't come. He would go off and forget his books, remembering them when he was sitting in class emptyhanded. He'd forget his lunch money and realize it when it was his break and his stomach was gnawing in hunger. If he forgot his bus ticket he'd have to either hitchhike or walk the long stretch home from high school.

So he started to remember! All by himself. When he finally realized no one was going to nag him and he had to count on himself, he became more responsible. This didn't happen overnight but at least it was a beginning.

One of the worst power struggles in my experience was of a mother and son who could never get up in time for school. The alarm would go off and he'd shut it off. Fifteen minutes later mother would come steaming down the hall, "Get up, get up, get up!"

It would always be "Just another minute."

"Get up, you're going to be late. Hurry up."

So, he'd pull the covers up over his head and go back to sleep. She come back screaming the second time, and the third. Finally he'd come staggering out, get halfway dressed, wash a little, hair half-combed and maybe get some breakfast. Maybe not, since he was always late.

I asked this young man if he liked waking up to this hassle every morning, waiting for his mother to come screaming at him. He admitted that he hated it. I asked him if he wanted to end it, and he said, "Well, I guess so."

So we decided on this strategy. He had a bad habit of going back to sleep after he had been awakened. I told him to get two alarm clocks, one by his bed and another one across the room. "Set them for one half hour before your mother comes tearing down the hallway. Now that's important. When the alarms go off and you have to get out of bed to shut off the second one, stay out of bed. Make it very quietly, go in and get washed, dressed and everything picked up as fast as you can. Then about the time you expect Mom, I want you to be sitting there on the edge of the bed, dressed with your hair combed. When she opens the door and yells, "Get up," you just say, "Morning, Mom, How're you today?"

That was a pleasant way to break up a stupid war. It's funny how long people will keep these things going, not stopping to realize there could be another way.

There is another area that absolutely blows my mind. I have parents who come in wanting to teach their son or daughter responsibility, and for some reason they have the belief that taking out the trash is character-building. If only we could get children to look for trash and take it out without being told, plus being thrilled to do it, then we would have a responsible human being! Sometimes I feel that if I have another parent come in saying their problem with their child is his unwillingness to take out the trash I'll just call it a day and go home.

I finally told one parent, "You're all upset because your son doesn't enjoy taking out the trash, when the truth of the matter is you don't want the responsibility either. You think this will make him responsible, taking out the trash? Do you really expect your son to go around the house saying, 'Oh boy, oh boy, there's some trash. Whoopee! I can't wait to pick up the trash. Oh boy, I'm going to be a trash collector!' Do you want him to be so turned on that he just can't help but look for trash. The only kid I ever knew who wanted to be a garbage collector did it to bug his parents because they kept saying that they wouldn't want their son to be a garbage collector. I don't mean that you can't ask your child to take out the trash. Just don't expect him to look forward to it. Tell him that taking out the trash is just being part of the family."

I know it's hard to find ways and means for young people to feel that they are contributing. We're not a rural community anymore where we have milking and chores; chickens and horses to feed, plowing and harvesting to be done. A young person, then, felt very needed and very much a part of that productive family. I think kids today feel somewhat obsolete. There are so few ways for them to contribute in a meaningful way which says, "Look, I'm important." Zeroing in on taking out the trash doesn't do the job. We make it tough for young people to find work by saying that they have to be sixteen in order to get a job.

The appearance of the bedroom has been a cause for much conflict between parent and teenager. I have the feeling that someone started the rumor years ago that the bedroom was owned by whoever slept in it; that he had a lease on it; that he could do with it as he pleased. No matter how dirty, how much it stunk, he could just jump out of his clothes, dump them, leave them on the floor and walk around them; eat food there and leave apple cores to rot. I don't know why we are so afraid of our child when he says, "Well, it's my room. I can do with it as I please."

A parent can say, "Wait a minute. Show me the lease or the deed. How much did you pay for that room?"

And he'll say, "Well, I didn't pay anything, but it's my room."

"Well, I'm sorry, but it isn't your room. Mom and Dad own this house and when you're old enough to own your own, you can live in it as dirty as you want. Right now we're concerned about the smell and disorder in your room. We have a right to be upset and it's up to you, since you don't own it, to keep it clean. We don't think that's too hard a job for you to do."

There are games children play with parents. I don't mean checkers and Monopoly, but hostile games. They learn them from watching us.

In An Uptight World

Here's a game that I've observed, along with other parents. A young person will want to do something, so he'll ask at the wrong time. He'll pick the time when his mother or father is most nervous and frazzled, worn out, or doing something very important. The child will come up and say "Can I do this?" or "Can I do that?" Parents have somehow learned how to say "No" before anything else and so "No" comes out without even thinking.

When the parent thinks about it afterwards, he realizes he shouldn't have said no, that the request really wasn't out of order, but he can't tell this to the child. The next time, the child comes up with a real "biggy", knowing that his parent still carries a little guilt over the last time. When he asks this time the parent says "Yes" whether he wants to or not, just because he said "No" so quickly the last time.

Parents have often discovered that if they try to please their children too much that *they* begin to run the house and rule them. They'll play one parent against the other every chance they get until the parents get smart and decide to do something about it. Let's be quite honest too. There isn't a parent alive who, if he wanted to do an in-depth study of his own *faux pas* and mistakes, couldn't find quite a bit of guilt. We all realize that we blew it several times but that doesn't mean that we can allow our children to push on our guilt button and get away with anything they want. I realize that parents become so bewildered and frightened of teenagers that

The Art Of Hanging Loose

I sometimes recommend a "spinal column implant." It helps them say "No" and stick to it. Remember this; when you say no to a child you must also give him the right to feel miserable.

Parents will also have to be alert that one child is not setting the other up to give him trouble with you. For instance, little ones poke, disturb, and smash toys of an older sibling. They do this very quietly and you don't always know it. All of a sudden you hear the older one screaming at the younger and then you scream at the older one, never stopping to find out what's really happening.

How does one go about talking about the period of adolescence without writing several volumes or a series of books? Because of the moods and changes and the powerful influences of their peer group, parents are baffled and puzzled about their son or daughter. Let's talk for awhile about fifteen-year-old boys and girls.

Fifteen—That Was a Very Bad Year

For some reason this seems to be a very troublesome year in the life of an adolescent. A boy begins to change emotionally and physically at about age thirteen. He becomes very conscious of authority and feels that he has a new sense of power in rebellion against authority. You can see him sitting in the 8th grade class with sullen eyes and trying to be Mr. Tough Guy and not listening to anything the teacher is saying. He is also somewhat puzzled and troubled with the strong sexual impulses he feels. Yet he doesn't know what to do with them.

At the same time he is going through a period of change, chaos and confusion. He tries to project the image of the super cool kid. He's new to the high school scene at fourteen and feels somewhat insecure about being low man on the totem pole after once being the big man in the 8th grade. He's no longer that awe-struck freshman nor that upper classman. He's insecure about being with parents and teachers. He covers all this insecurity about who he is with an arrogant brashness. The truth is that down beneath he's really not a so-called "cool kid".

He'd like to get a job and earn some money to buy a car, but no one wants to hire him since he's not sixteen.

He'd like to date but he's tired of dad offering to pick up his girl, take them to the movies, and bring them home. He looks around for a girl his own age and all of a sudden they seem much more mature and aware and they frighten and frustrate him. Suddenly the only way he feels that he can talk to a girl is via the telephone, mumbling his "Wow", "Man" and "Far Out", with long pauses. He's learning and it's hard. Then if he does have the courage to ask a girl out, she says she's sorry but she's going with so and so who is 16 or 17 or 18 and has wheels and more money to spend.

His physical growth sometimes causes him great

feelings of awkwardness and self-consciousness. And what is he going to do about pimples and the changing voice and the emotional floundering?

He has feelings of both love and frustration about his parents. He's afraid to express his feeling of love for fear they might really control him again, and so he acts as if nobody can tell him what to do.

His friends become his preoccupation. Collectively, they decide what the styles are to be, where to go, what to do and how to kill time. They blame others for life being so boring. Actually, it's a very comforting experience. They talk about automobiles, music and sports. You get the idea that he doesn't dare think differently from the group because that might make him an outsider.

He looks at the world through inverted eyeballs. His parents are worried about his lack of responsibility, his forgetfulness. He vacillates in his moods and desires. One day he wants to raise fish and the next day birds. The next day he doesn't want to raise anything.

Now, what happens to girls? Fifteen can be a very bad year for them also, only sometimes it starts earlier, around twelve. They begin to mature physically and emotionally. Listen to your daughter when she talks to you, because suddenly their girl friends of many years standing can suddenly turn on them and as a group become very cruel, jealous and vicious. If your daughter is a winner others will try to put her down with gossip, two against one. If she is too outstanding then she is a threat, even to her best friend.

The seventh and eighth grade years can be very devastating to both girls and boys. You must listen to the moods and hurts of your children, but don't always think that they are angry with you. Maybe she's afraid to tell you that she's hurting inside and doesn't think she can make it with all the pressures. Yet she's reluctant to mention it in her fear that you'll be upset; that you'll wonder what's wrong with her that she can't get along with the others. She doesn't want you to think less of her.

Girls become very flirtatious. Mothers become very threatened. What has happened to this nice little girl who was so obedient and sweet in a pinafore dress? Now she wants to go braless and talks in a lingo that you don't approve of. She used to be so neat, and now sloppiness is the in thing. The girl is growing so fast and changing unbelieveably. Physically she is ready to become a mother but emotionally she still very much needs a mother.

One bit of advice I can give to parents of children this age is to remember the generation boundary. Please be a parent; not a pal, or a peer, or a competitor. At those times I find the most confused people of all are the teenagers, especially girls. A mother will start off the morning trying to be a mother with, "Here's your lunch money." Then the girl brings her boyfriend home after school and her mother suddenly acts like a sister and wants to flirt with the boy. When the girl comes from a broken home the mother will often ask approval of her daughter to go out on a date. It's enough to drive a teenager crazy—three changes in one day— mother to daughter, peer to peer, and now her being a parent of mother.

I guess I'm one of the few people who say 'hooray' for the generation boundary. It can provide much security, especially with girls. Don't feel threatened that you have to compete with them because they're young. Would you really want to be fifteen again, or have you amnesia for that period of your life? Weren't you afraid and worried about what others were thinking of you; what other girls were saying; having fantasies of people always talking about you. Fortunately, that's not true. They don't talk that much but you can't convince a teenager of this fact.

Young girls can become very snappy and cruel with their mother because she's not "in" with the styles like her friends are. Mothers, on the other hand, are disgusted with what her daughter wants to buy at the department store because either it looks like something Groucho Marx would pick for a comedy routine or something her grandmother wore when she was a little girl. And the struggle and arguments go on.

Is there hope for those who are fifteen? Yes, one day they will become sixteen, and then seventeen. Just hang in there and hang loose. Remember, above all they still need your love and your listening, and your firm, consistent boundaries. Don't give up your spinal column, and don't give up your hugging them. You can't choose all of their friends and you can't make every decision for them, so come to terms with the realities of your limitations and of what you can do.

Teenagers also have a culture that is beyond our understanding or control, a culture that is preaching subversive values. "Do your own thing. It's your life so don't let anyone tell you what to do. Who wants to work 9 to 5 every day? Who wants to be a jock and get good grades?" The pressure to conform is great because of their fragmented egos most young people are not ready to pay the price of individuality. It's not easy being your own person at fifteen.

The drug culture is a real threat and fear. It has struck across our country. The drug epidemic really exploded during 1968 and 1969. It was during that time that I started a group in Phoenix called *Parents Anonymous*. The sole purpose was for it to be a self-help group for parents who suddenly discovered one of their children was using drugs. It was a place where they could come and know that each one in the room had a similar problem. They could talk in small groups and help themselves and develop their own panic line.

Dr. Spock didn't tell us in his book what we should do when we find our child is on drugs. Drugs were always connected with ghetto kids but never with children from our good homes! Some of our greatest universities are the leading drug-oriented schools in this country.

Youth Headed for Trouble

As a therapist specializing in teenagers, two ingredients have been very important to me. One is to be myself, and the other is to always be truthful. I also know I have to go the third mile with love, even for some of those who are pretty unlovable.

Young people headed for trouble have one tape that you find very common. It's an Anti-Authority tape that may be expressed in anti-establishment and anti-society, but it is basically the thought, "No one can tell me what to do." When someone tries to tell him what to do, other than a peer, it automatically pushes his tape and he rejects whatever you have to say, even if he believes as you do. It must be rejected because it came from someone in authority. He's always waiting for somebody to push his button so he can react. It's a rather sad way to live.

Let me give you an illustration of how pointless this behavior is. Several years ago I had therapy for some boys in a halfway house. Each of these boys had been sentenced to the state reformatory or the state prison with his sentence suspended, provided he made it in the halfway house. He had to get a job, go to school and live by the rules of the home. One day before a group, a young man came in absolutely livid with rage and swearing at the director of the home.

"Cool it, Bill. What's your problem?"

"That blankety-blank so-and-so said I had to cut my hair."

"So what's the deal? You knew what the house rules were. You have to have your hair a certain length to get employed. That's nothing new. It beats being locked up."

"Well, nobody's going to tell me what to do. I'll go to Fort Grant (the state reformatory) before I'll cut my hair!"

"Hey, wait a minute, stupid. Answer me this question. If your best buddy asked you to cop a crime that he did, say you did it and spend two years in prison for it, just because you're buddies, would you do it?"

"You've got to be crazy, Doc. I wouldn't do that. What do you think I am, stupid?"

And I said, 'Yes, I think you're stupid with your thinking. If you wouldn't go to Fort Grant for a friend, why would you be willing to go for your enemy? What would you prove? They'd cut your hair and give you blue dungarees. After all, Billy, it's only protein, but two years is two years".

Billy stopped to think it over and realized that he was being pretty stupid. By the way, there is always hope for the world when man begins to think instead of just to react or play a negative tape.

I hadn't seen him for years, and then one day on my way to the crime lab I heard a voice call out, "Hey, Doc." and there was Billy. He told me things had been going great for him. He was married and had two children of his own. He was very thankful for the day I stopped him from making a big mistake.

There is what I call a 'muttonhead psychology' behind the acting out, delinquent, drug behavior. Some years ago in Arizona great herds of sheep would be driven to the northern country to escape the summer heat. Intermingled with these herds of sheep you found many goats. Their purpose was to lead the flocks up the mountain paths. If a sheep went off a cliff, and there wasn't a goat to lead them away, the other sheep would simply follow the one who had fallen. It's this muttonhead kind of psychology, 'everyone's doing it', that causes so many people so much grief.

What about discipline versus punishment? Discipline is a concept that means to learn. I've used this theory, and I'm sure others have also, in dealing with troubled boys and girls. They sometimes act impulsively and then say, "But I didn't think!" I say, "That's right." Discipline works this way.

While I was a consulting psychologist for a residential girls' home the group worked out its own self-management and self-governing concepts. The goal was to break up the institutional atmosphere of the delinquents versus the staff. I was able to convince the staff and the girls that if they were ever going to achieve any kind of personal responsibility for their lives and quit playing the "blame game",

they would have to start being responsible by owning up to their own mistakes and breaking up the
contract. The contract means, "I won't tell on you
and you won't tell on me if you're doing something
against the law or stupid." When someone acted out
or did something stupid the girls would get together
and work out what kind of discipline she should do.

Here's how it worked. I know this may seem a
little extreme but sometimes people need extremes
to help them think and remember, so they won't be
so unthinking next time. Two new girls came into
the home and were welcomed by two of the girls
who had been there awhile. They were greeted with
a message like this:

"We know that you two have been locked up for
some time. You think it's nicer in this house where
you can get out the front door, sneak away and
really act up, and do something dumb. But you
should know the house rules. We all like it here
and we also want you to know that we won't cover
for you and not tell if you break the rules. That
doesn't help you grow up. If you do something
stupid the group will work out a discipline with
you."

These two girls didn't believe them at all, because
the very first night they quietly left. They stole some
rum, got very drunk and one was arrested for being
drunk and disorderly. The next day the group met
and, needless to say, there was a very heavy confron-
tation about their behavior. So they negotiated with

the girls. The new girls were asked what they thought would make them remember next time, and the group came up with this discipline. For a period of five days each week, two hours a day, the girls would dig a hole 3' x 3' deep. When it was dug to that dimension the girls on discipline would both contemplate how stupid their behavior was. This they did for two weeks. One of the girls decided to get smart in a hurry.

Once in a while you see a breakthrough. We had "owning up" time during some of our sessions. That meant you own up to what you have been doing wrong and stupid. You can't carry guilt around because it shows in your face and the atmosphere in the home gets too tense because of the guilty people. This particular girl, who had been one of the leaders and prize pupils, said she had to own up to something.

"I got stoned last weekend on my home pass."

We were all hurt and somewhat dismayed because she had been doing so well. The group began to discuss her discipline. What would best help her remember to say "No" to herself.

She said, "You can't take my home visit away this weekend, because I have a boyfriend coming over from California."

We let it ride at that and the group began to discuss with her the many and sundry disciplines, from scrubbing the kitchen floor with a toothbrush to how long she should clean toilet bowls and so on down the line.

I finally turned to her and said. "When you first came here I asked you what you needed most of all to change. You said that you'd always been able to get away with anything you wanted with your parents. They could never say no to you so you did everything and anything you pleased. You said you needed to learn to say no to yourself. We know that it's hard to say no to yourself. What of all these disciplines do you think would help you finally learn?"

She thought a moment and said, "I know I need help. I'll have to give up my weekend pass. Only that would be hard enough to make me think next time."

The group started to say, "Oh, that's too tough."

I said, "No. Wait a minute. Don't defend her. She knows what she needs and sometimes it's doing that which is hard that saves our lives."

From that point on she did very well.

The basic difference between discipline and punishment is that discipline is mutually agreed upon by all parties involved, whereas when a person is punished he has no say in his punishment. He only receives the punishment and often feels that the punishment was not fair, so it provides him with an excuse to do something stupid at a later time.

One time a boy was in trouble with his school for smoking in the boys' bathroom. He was expelled for two days. He had no talent for crime but he didn't know it at that time, and was already messed up. I just couldn't get over this latest incidence.

The Art Of Hanging Loose

"I just couldn't help it, Doc. The impulse just came over me that I had to have a cigarette so I went in and smoked one and was caught. I just wasn't thinking."

"That's right. You don't think, do you?"

"No, I didn't."

"I believe you need some time to think."

We sat down to work out a discipline. It started on Christmas Day and would last the entire Christmas Holidays. He would spend every afternoon at the high school parking lot, picking up cigarette butts. He was to pick each cigarette butt up and smell it and remember his stupidity so that he would think next time before doing something rash. He agreed with me that this was a reasonable discipline. That was the secret. He had to agree to it or it wouldn't work.

You should see the photo taken of him that vacation with his huge bag full of cigarette butts. That was the last time he was kicked out of school for smoking in the boys' bathroom.

The Joy of the Hassle-Free Life

Do you know what the real payoff is for young people who have been in trouble? Do you know what makes them feel the best of all? It's the hassle-free life. This happens when he no longer is confused about who he is because he has found himself and leveled with the world.

Now very often I'll hear something like this from a young person. "Doc, you can't imagine how good I feel inside and what a relief to get rid of the load of a guilty conscience. It's great to not be so uptight and wondering when I'll get caught in my next lie. What a relief to not have to worry about a police car coming down the street and get paranoid as to whether or not I'll get busted. It's wonderful to feel alive again after living such a boring and dull existence. I had perfected the art of doing nothing as a life style."

To be able to look at yourself in the mirror and feel a sense of pride and accomplishment through success at school or holding a job, then have people say, "You're doing great", is a rewarding experience. The greatest gift from the hassle-free life for a young person is that for once he can say, "I'm proud of me," and this feels good.

How to Solve the Problem of School Successfully

This is a little special section for young people. I realize that perhaps you might think I'm a very tough, hardnosed therapist, and I *am*, with hardnosed, tough kids. But I also love them and go out on a limb for them. I don't always believe I have to win but I do believe I have to be there to try *one more* time. I know your parents are no doubt saying, "Now read this part of the book. Read it right now," and you're telling them you don't want to read it.

The Art Of Hanging Loose

Just forget about your parents for a moment and listen to some of my secrets. If you're having trouble with school I have a few helpful hints on how to solve the problem successfully, without a lot of hassle, war and wasted time. Individuals who have trouble with school often play a negative tape called, "I Hate School". This tape is filled with thoughts of teachers and memories and emotions of times when you have stood up in front of class and tried to read and kids laughed at you. Maybe you've had this experience or perhaps you've just gotten sullen and given up on yourself. If you're playing and thinking the "I Hate School" tape how can anything good come from school or learning into your awareness until you turn off the tape?

If you'd like to solve the problem of school successfully here are a few ground rules. In order that you don't bum your head out with negative tapes you must begin to accept a few facts. No one said you had to like school, like the teachers or like any particular subject, and that's part of the problem. You've probably been told all your life that you have to go to school to learn facts and get an education. From my point of view the purpose of education is to teach you how to solve life's problems so you end up winning and feeling good about yourself, instead of losing and being miserable. If school, teachers, subjects, and the peers are the ingredients that go into making problems, how are you going to go about solving them successfully?

First of all, take a look at the opposite extreme—the person who doesn't solve the problem successfully. Very often I have parents come to me with children who are failing. I'll never forget one family. The father felt his girls didn't amount to much. They weren't very bright so he never bothered with their education or put pressure upon them. They did quite well in high school and college. However, he felt boys had to be smart, great talented, industrious and educated. From the first day they went to school he was on their backs. They reacted, instead of acting in their behalf and because of the pressure they became those who did not solve the school problem successfully. They became the failures. They'd do anything to keep from winning to make their father right. One day I asked the young man who was failing, "How do you go about failing? What's your plan?"

"What do you mean, what's my plan?"

"Well, you've got a plan because it works so beautifully. You flunk, or darn near flunk every time. Now that takes a certain amount of planning. Now how do you go about planning to flunk or get bad grades?"

"Well," he said, "I don't go to class too often and when I'm there I sort of daydream and sleep. I don't turn in many of my assignments."

"That's a beautiful plan and it's really working."

"And I never study for a test."

"That's right, because if you study you might

blow it and get a C and ruin the whole thing. It works. The plan works and you get D's and F's. It's a great plan to fail. Now, how do you feel about it. How do you feel inside?"

"What do you mean?" he wanted to know.

"Well, how do you feel about being such a good failure?"

"Terrible. Just terrible".

I asked him if he'd like to know how to solve the problem of school without wasting so much time and make the time go faster. He wanted to do that. Here are some of the guidelines I offer to solve the problem of school successfully.

All right, first of all you accept the fact that you'll have to be there for the hour anyway. And if you try to waste the hour away it drags, doesn't it? Minutes seem like hours, and it just goes on and on. Why don't you move up to the front of the class and tell yourself that you'll listen in order to solve the problem of this teacher. Find out what he or she feels is important. If he gives you a clue to what he thinks is important, make a note of it and put an 'x' by it and be sure to study that particular thing. When you move to the front of the room you are sitting right up by the teacher and you're asking for answers that you need to know. The teacher thinks, 'My, here is an eager student.' The teacher doesn't know he's just helping do homework for you, plus giving you individualized instruction. This is how the time passes faster. You don't have to worry so much about school when you go home.

Another thing, when you have a textbook with questions at the end of the chapter, *this* is where you start. Read the first question. Then go back to the beginning of the chapter and search until you find the answer, and make a mark or the numeral one. Follow this procedure with each of the following questions. Notice that you have not read the chapter as yet, but now as you do read it you are not wondering what the most important parts are because you have already highlighted them. This is also a time-saver in reviewing several chapters in preparation for a test. If you want to increase the effectiveness of your time in the classroom, read one chapter ahead of the class assignment. Then when that material is discussed in class it will already be familiar to you and you can ask intelligent questions.

One of the worst habits for many students, as well as adults in general, is that of procrastination. When a person knows there is something to do, something to be finished, but the task is delayed, he's hounded by the nagging worry and frustration of the incompleted job. You'll begin to realize what a parasite this is. Even when you should be having fun you're plagued with worry about the unfinished business. Someone once said that worry is like a rocking chair. It gives you something to do but you never go anywhere.

Procrastination is a habit that can be broken. For example, when a teacher assigns a special paper to be done, don't wait until the night before and then become very frustrated. Naturally, the end product is not of good quality. I discovered that when a teacher gave the assignment to do a special report, it was much easier to begin work on it when it was assigned and to finish the paper well in advance of the deadline. It is no mystery that other teachers will also ask you to do extra reports, so if you don't work fast you can be forced to do several at one time. Develop the habit of doing assignments as soon as possible and then you'll never get behind in your course work. You'll then discover that when you have fun, it is a hassle-free time from school work. Give your brain a rest and hang loose. If you do these things you'll deserve to have a good time.

Perhaps I shouldn't write this section, because you can imagine how it would blow teachers' minds suddenly to have the chronic "D" and "F" student start doing "A" and "B" work. It might keep them awake at night wondering what happened to that bored, dull, student. Can't you just see a group of them talking in the faculty lounge, wondering what happened to dumb John. First of all they may feel he's cheating, but no one can report seeing him cheat. They're left with the mystery of the miracle of the transformation of a borderline or failing student into a superior student who now knows how to solve the problem of school successfully.

The next step is called three-dimensional learning. Too often a student uses only one dimension of learning through reliance on sight retention of new learning. If you can visualize the mind as a memory bank with tapes that receive and store new information through imprints being made on the tape, then sight alone will make a weak imprint. The second dimension is through the use of your muscles. For example, when you write an outline for a chapter, or write a list of definitions of terms on paper, the imprint of the information is recorded with greater clarity and this makes recall of this much easier. The third dimension is that of saying out loud what it is you want to learn so now the acoustical dimension will make an even better imprint on the tape that is stored in your mind's memory bank. I have often wondered why teachers have not encouraged students to study together after school. Do you realize that if a group of friends began to talk and question each other about the course material to be recalled for a test that there would be much more information retained, plus the fun of solving the problem with some good friends. This increases learning, makes it more fun and is a great timesaver. A study group also encourages each person to do better.

Snowball learning is another technique which may be helpful for someone who is having a difficult time with a particular subject. Let's say a student is struggling with a foreign language. The first step is to buy a package of 3 x 5 cards and cut them into four pieces, or whatever size you wish. Write down the various verb conjugations in the foreign language on one side and the English translations on the other side. Record other vocabulary words in the same manner. Put a handful of these cards in your pocket or purse.

During the day when you have a spare minute quickly review them until you can separate those which you know from those on which you still need to work a little more. This doesn't take much time, but if you do it daily, a few minutes at a time, you begin to snowball the knowledge. What started out as just a little knowledge begins to grow and grow like a snowball grows as it rolls down the hill.

Remember, don't waste your mental energy on the negative tapes "I hate school" or "I hate the teacher" or a certain subject. This doesn't help solve the problem, and all it accomplishes is you making yourself miserable and uptight.

Don't be like the high school junior who came to me because he was failing general mathematics for the third year and he needed a math credit to graduate. His excuse was that he just 'hated' general math.

I said, "I thought you were trying to major in general math for four years. You're the first kid I've ever seen who was trying so successfully to not pass a course so he could take it year after year."

"Doc, I can't stand the thought of taking it again next year."

"Well," I said, "at the rate you're going I can almost visualize you as a senior greeting this new little freshman by saying, 'Welcome to general math. Old 'teach' and I know each other real well because we're together for the fourth year now!"

The point I tried to make with him was that he didn't have to *like* general math to pass it. If he had to have it for credit to graduate then didn't it make sense to pass the subject and get rid of it instead of taking it over and over again? He finally saw the light and decided to pass whether he liked it or not.

How to Retire from Being a Parent

There have been thousands of books written and millions of words spoken on how to be a parent. Apparently no one has ever gotten around to saying, "When do you quit. When do you retire?" There is no question that our main problem is that we have parented our children for so many years that the parent-child relationship becomes habituated to the point of a reflex action. So much love, energy, worry, and wear and tear goes into the raising of a child that it's hard for us to realize that there comes a point in time when the child is an adult and the years of parenting the child are over. Now is the time to retire from the role of being a parent. Since none of us are perfect as individuals, much less as parents, there is a feeling arising out of guilt that perhaps there is one more thing to tell a son or daughter. There is also the fear that if a child makes a mistake in life it is automatically a reflection on the quality of job the parents did in rearing the child. So, parents continue to hang in with advice-giving and guidance. It really doesn't matter how old the children are. I'm sure that even if you are a parent yourself, and responsible adult, doing a fine job with your own children, a strange feeling comes over you when you visit your parents. All of a sudden at your forty or fifty-odd years of age you discover that *your* parent is relating to you in a parent-child relationship. You share some news and you receive correction or advice for what you *should* have done. This can be infuriating as well as frustrating to you, but remember, no one ever taught them how to retire from the role of being a parent.

How *do* you retire? I have no final solution to the problem, but I do offer these few suggestions which may help you discover more answers on your own. While a child is growing begin to retire by allowing him to participate in decision making. Expand the areas for more personal responsibility for his own behavior. Don't become easily threatened if your son or daughter is expressing a point of view different from your own. Remember, the young adult is more at home in the world of today than his parents, but as a parent you still have the advantage through the years of experiencing life in all its many ups and downs. Start listening to yourself to see if you are still trying to communicate with your offspring by lecturing with a number of "shoulds" and "oughts" and old clichés thrown in for good measure. The need to listen is more apparent than ever. You must reach the point that you can admit to yourself that there is nothing new you can say that will make any difference. That's the time you will relax and retire from being a parent, enjoying your relationship to one another as adults. Your child is no longer a child but a young man or woman, who will establish an identity in his or her own right. Now parents can spend more time, money and energy enjoying their marriage and the freedom of not being parents anymore.

My wife's parents intuitively knew how to retire from their role. When we were married they never gave us any advice or told us what to do. From that day on they only related to us as adults, and did not interfere in our lives. For that and many other reasons, I am eternally grateful.

8

Strictly Personal

I started out in this book talking about our living in an uptight world, and I offered some ways to learn the art of hanging loose. The real issue for you and for me, though, is one of our own personal philosophy of life. What an individual believes about himself, the world, and other people will determine how he will live his life.

If a person has incongruous and even conflicting beliefs and values, then his life will reveal his inner confusion and inconsistencies. For the individual who has never struggled with and come to terms with the "who" that I am, and the "why and what" that I am, his life will be rather pointless and empty. His theme song will be, "Is That All There Is?"

The Art Of Hanging Loose

It is not easy to learn patience; to be still and look within yourself; to risk taking off all the masks that you hide behind; to end the destructive games with people. But I believe that if an individual can do such a pilgrimage into self, what he will find will not be that he is so bad, but that he is so rich in unused potential; that he has a great capacity to love and become alive.

I am often asked by people, "But if I get rid of all my negative tapes, what will I put in the vacuum left in my life?" This is not a trite question. If an individual has lived a very negative life and if most of his perceptions have been selected to respond to the negatives in people and the world, then to give up or turn off his negative tapes is asking him to radically change his personality. The answer is simple and hard. Into the vacuum left by the negative tapes you place LOVE. You can learn to love as you learn to be negative. A person can learn new behavior as long as he lives.

I would like to share with you a little of my life and some of my own hangups and personal beliefs. I don't know whether it was because I was the middle child of five children or that I was born in 1930 in the midst of the depression, but I believed that I had to prove myself worthy. As I look back on my life I realize that I was striving for my father's approval. He was a very hard worker, so I decided I would prove to him that I, too, was a hard worker. During the summer of my 14th year I went with a friend to a cement block factory to see if we could get a job stacking blocks. We watched five men lazily stack the blocks and decided that the two of us could do the job much faster than the five men. Thus, I boldly approached one of the owners of the factory and said, "Dad . . . . "

Well, the truth is that we were hired and we proved without any doubt that we could do the work much faster than the five men. Each summer after that I worked in the cement block factory and was determined to save my money to pay my own way through college.

Since I do a great deal of public speaking and have done so for many years, when I tell an audience that as a teenager I was very shy and bashful with people they don't believe me; but it was true. I was so afraid of speaking up that when I met a new person I mumbled a lot.

In fact, when I met a person I never looked them in the eye, but always looked at their shoes—like saying "Hello, brown shoes," or "Hello, black shoes, how are you?" I used to believe that when I walked into a room full of people, that every eye was upon me. And then one day I was shocked when I had the courage and peeked. I discovered that no one was looking at me!

One thing I did want to do was play football. From the time I was six-years-old that was my dream. I couldn't wait to get to high school to play football. Now I didn't have the great natural talents and ability that a great many athletes have, so I had to work harder.

Our coach during my senior year in high school had to be, without a doubt, one of the most inspirational men in my life, and also one of the most feared in my life. His name was Walt Ruth. His life had been hard. He had come up and fought for everything in his life, but he believed if you tried hard and worked hard you could play football for him. He had a discipline that you wouldn't believe. He was the Vince Lombardi of high school football.

If you sat down during practice, you ran 26 laps —that's a little over six miles. If you began to fumble too often you ran 26 laps. In Arizona we had a joke during the game when there was a time-out, and the referee said you could have the water boy come on. That always cracked us up because we didn't have a water boy!

When he said, "Jump!" you said, "How high?" Well, in one of the first games of the year I was playing defensive right halfback. The end from the opposing team caught a pass behind me for a touchdown and they won the game. I was devastated and apologized to the coach and the team. And wouldn't you know, in the Sunday morning paper there was a picture of me desperately leaping into the air trying to knock down the pass while the end was catching it for a touchdown. Well, I dreaded Monday morning because I knew there would be a call for me to meet with Walt Ruth during PE and this was like waiting to meet your executioner, your policeman your judge, all in one. I went to his office. They didn't need to open the door. I just walked underneath it, I felt so low. There on his desk, sure enough, was the picture from Sunday's paper. He looked at me with his square jaw and piercing eyes and said, "What do you have to say about this picture."

I said, "Coach, I am really sorry, I'll try harder next time."

He said, "Look at that picture again. Look at your face. Look at your muscles. Can't you see that's your problem? You try too hard. Now, if I had everyone on this team trying as hard as you do all the time there isn't a high school team in the country that we couldn't beat. Now would you please just relax and believe in yourself and you'll be a great ball player."

Walt Ruth was known as a hard, tough coach. But through the years the young boys learned to respect him, and later as men to feel a sense of gratitude for knowing a man like Walt Ruth. He had the ability to inspire belief in yourself. It helps to have somebody say, "I believe in you. Hang loose."

And as far as the record goes, I believe that was about the last pass that was ever caught in my area for the rest of the season because of the power to relax and believe in myself knowing that someone else believed also.

My compulsion to prove myself did result in my accomplishing a great deal in my life, but I still was looking over my shoulder as if to say, "Dad, am I good enough yet?" The end result of my compulsion was that I became a work addict.

Finally one day when I was twenty-eight-years-old I came to terms with the motives behind my drive; to realize it was based on my need for acceptance. I made the decision that I could accept myself as I was. I admitted I wasn't perfect but I was all right and I had accomplished a great deal in my life even if the motivation had not been the best. I also realized that my father was human and maybe he could not give that approval or acceptance I needed. Maybe that was his problem, and not mine. When I could accept myself, the whole me with faults and good qualities I found an inner peace. This experience made it clear to me what it means to be accepted, forgiven and loved by God. In spite of all the sermons I had preached on God's love, now finally I could understand it because I experienced this great love and acceptance.

Man is so proud, and we always like to think we have to prove ourselves good enough and worthy enough so that people and God will accept us. I finally discovered that God's love is greatly different from human love. He comes to us on the basis not that we earned it or deserve it or have the brownie points or the perfect attendance records, but offers us love because we need it. He comes to us because we are messed up; that we'll never be perfect; and He loves us, accepts us and forgives us. He knows all that there is to know about us so nothing is hidden from Him. I think love and acceptance can help us to become what we are truly meant to be.

For me, I try to express it, sometimes not too successfully because I'm human. As a life of Thanksgiving I give thanks for the love I have already received and the acceptance I have already experienced, and the forgiveness that is there. And I even figured out that if God could forgive me and love me and accept me, maybe I could even forgive myself and not try to upstage Him. If I could do that I could change. If I look at another person and realize he's got faults like mine I'll accept that person as he is because we are just folks. Maybe I can share a little love and a little huggin' to let them know that they are OK, too.

Frankly, I'm a hugger. I like to hug people. Come to think of it, it's really a nice hobby.

There was one time when I was a little concerned about my hugging. One day as I came out of my private office and stepped into the waiting room I saw an old friend of mine who had come to Phoenix from the University of Arizona in Tucson. He had just wanted to drop by and say "Hi". He had been one of the ex-addicts who had worked with me when I was the director of a drug treatment center in Phoenix. We instinctively gave each other a great big hug just because we were so glad to see each other.

Waiting for the next appointment was a mother and her son who was just ten years old. They were there to see me for the first time. When they came back the next week I asked to see the mother alone for a moment. I was curious about the reaction of her ten-year-old son when he saw two men hugging each other.

"Oh", she replied, "he was quite impressed with you. He said any doctor can't be too bad if he can hug a longhair."

I believe in love. I believe in music and I believe that each bird whistles through his own beak. The rare uniqueness of each individual is a marvel to behold. What a mistake parents make when they want their children to be carbon copies of themselves or extensions of themselves instead of marveling at the uniqueness of each of their children and encouraging them to express their own uniqueness, their "you-ness".

What a dull world if all people, plants and days were the same! The true task of education is to draw out the uniqueness within each person instead of trying to pour into their lives what someone else believes *should be* put into a student. If we discover someone's dissimilarity, don't rush to judgment because the other is not like us. Listen to their thoughts, and grow and change through the encounter.

I believe in being rigidly flexible. That strange statement means that I believe in setting goals for myself and once I have decided what they are then I can hang loose and be very flexible in trying many ways to reach those goals. If I encounter obstacles and barriers, then I have the opportunity to use them as a "honing stone". These make me sharper to be more flexible in overcoming the barriers. I can fail but I am not a failure.

In fact, being a psychotherapist has taught me to have a high tolerance for failure, knowing that there is only so much I can do with another person. He can always reject whatever advice or help I may offer. Since I know I can't be successful every time, I have come to terms with this. What I ask of myself is to be there when needed and be willing to try one more time.

I believe in being truthful with people so I don't get confused and they will always know where I stand. I speak the truth in love and sometimes with hard-core people I speak the truth in love, but very bluntly.

I believe in hanging loose emotionally. The art of hanging loose emotionally is an art because few people do it naturally. Most of us have to work very hard learning how to turn off our negative tapes and cut loose the bad memories, hurts, disappointments and bitterness of yesterday. It's hard to walk away from the bad memories of yesterday because, for some strange reason, individuals believe if they can spend enough time on yesterday's mistakes and hurts that yesterday will be different. But we cannot get from here to yesterday and do a remake of it, so why hang onto the bummers of the past? They'll just drag you down emotionally. I discovered that in my life I could not afford the distinctive luxury of hate or bitterness. It's far too expensive a price for me to pay.

When I was about four or five I discovered that tomorrow never comes. When I would ask my mother for something she would reply, "Well, maybe tomorrow we can do it," but the next day wasn't tomorrow, it was today. So, if you and I can't go back to yesterday or live in tomorrow, I believe we should spend more energy in living more fully and completely the day that we have.

Don't wait to share your love. If you want to enjoy a richer life, begin each day wondering who you can touch or love or hug, or make someone think they are for real.

On a skiing trip a friend of mine and I stopped at the top of a mountain to go into a refreshment hut for some hot cider. My companion gave the waiter a tip and said to him, "Thanks for being here." That didn't take much of an effort or even cost much, but the surprised smile on the waiter's face said it all.

Life is what you are looking for. If you are searching for everything that's wrong with people and the world, that's what you'll find. You will then prove to yourself that the world and it's people are no good. But, if you look for the gold in those around you, your life will be rich in friends.

I realize that I have an advantage over most people because I live in this beautiful desert of Arizona, where the sunrises and sunsets are never the same. I never tire of the beauty of it. I believe life is so exciting, so marvelous that I'll never have enough time to retire because there is always one more thing to learn—one more person to meet and hug—and a never-ending stream of ideas to follow through on.

I'm going to close this chapter with a quotation from the book *Journey to Ixtlan** by Carlos Castaneda. This is a conversation between Don Juan, a Yaqui sorcerer and Carlos, who is trying to become a sorcerer. Carlos is a university professor of anthropology. Don Juan is speaking.

> *"One must assume responsibility for being in a weird world," he said. "We are in a weird world, you know."*
>
> *I nodded my head affirmatively.*
>
> *"We're not talking about the same thing," he said, "For you the world is weird because if you're not bored with it you're at odds with it. For me the world is weird because it is stupendous, awesome, mysterious, unfathomable; my interest has been to convince you that you must assume responsibility for being here, in this marvelous world, in this marvelous desert, in this marvelous time. I wanted to convince you that you must learn to make every act count, since you are going to be here for only a short while, in fact, too short for witnessing all the marvels of it."*

*Pg. 107, *JOURNEY TO IXTLAN*, The Lessons of Don Juan, Carlos Castaneda. Simon and Schuster.

Psychological Exercises

Exploring Your Past

1. How do you feel about your name and nick-name?

2. What are some earliest memories? Pleasant and unpleasant.

3. What is your greatest fear?

4. Of what are you most proud about yourself? Remember this is about you, not someone else such as your children.

5. What messages did you receive from your parents or other significant adults in your life about the following topics—remember, these messages are mostly non-verbal:

- (a) Showing affection, like hugging.
- (b) Work
- (c) Play
- (d) Sex
- (e) Conditional love or unconditional love.
- (f) School and report cards
- (g) Showing emotions such as anger, sorrow, joy, etc.
- (h) What was the favorite saying, or words to live by of each of your parents?
- (i) What about the importance of a religious life?
- (j) What did your parents do for fun?
- (k) What did they believe about discipline?

6. How did you handle or feel about important changes that took place in your family life such as the following:

- (a) Death in the family
- (b) Moving to a new place
- (c) Birth of another child
- (d) Divorce
- (e) Re-marriage
- (f) Step-parents
- (g) Step-brothers, sisters or children
- (h) Other problems such as an alcoholic parent or an emotionally unstable parent

7. School—a large part of your growing years were spent here.

    (a) Who was your favorite teacher and what was your favorite subject?

    (b) Who was your worst teacher and what was your most difficult subject?

    (c) What did you like most about school?

    (d) What did you like least about school?

    (e) Did you give up on yourself at times and say "I can't. I hate school"?

    (f) What did you learn about learning?

    (g) How much do you read and what types of books?

    (h) Have you ever wanted to write a story or poetry? Why not?

    (i) What would you like to learn now?

Fantasy Games

1. **The Magic Store.** Imagine that you are going into this magic store which is filled with things you can't buy in any other store. The shelves are filled with a variety of items, and in this store are some things that, if you had them, would make you feel great. For instance: Perhaps you are shy. Well, look around and find the item called self-confidence. There *is* one rule. To obtain one of these items you

must give up something in you and place it in a refuse can. For example: In the refuse can the shy person would put his shyness. This is lots of fun to do with a small group. You must imagine how what you select will feel and how it will change your life.

2. **The Last People on Earth.** You are one of a small group of people who are going to leave the civilized world and live on a tropical island in the South Pacific. Since you will be the only humans left on earth you will be able to take with you a few things before you start your new life. Each person can decide what he prefers from the following ideas:

(a) What five books would you bring?
(b) What five miscellaneous articles would you bring?
(c) What five sources of food would you bring?
(d) If you could add one more person to your group, who would it be and why?
(e) To keep your minds active you develop thinking games to construct theories. There is no right or wrong theory but the goal is to develop creative thinking on subjects like the following:
Why does a coconut float, or need to float?
What is the purpose of wind?
How would you go about living to an age of one hundred?

How do you send thoughts to another person?

Develop your ideas on subjects to theorize about.

3. **Group Mystery or Adventure Story.**

(a) Each person in a small group must first pick a character in the story and tell the group about what kind of a person he is, how old, his good points and weaknesses, so a characterization is developed.
(b) The group then decides the major plot, where the story takes place, what period of history, or if it is science fiction, even better.
(c) Each person follows the other so when one starts the story then stops the next one picks up and continues. It is added fun to have a tape recorder for this new, exciting, creative story.

Personal Inventory

1. What resentments do you have now. Make a list of them and then evaluate the need to keep them or release them by deciding to let go of the resentments. Who needs bitterness?

2. Are you able to admit to yourself and others that you have been wrong and can you go to the

offended person and ask for forgiveness. Try it. It's painful but very conducive to personal growth.

3. What things have you done in the past that you find hard to forgive yourself? If you can't forgive yourself, are you trying to upstage God when He is willing to forgive you?

4. Do you find yourself yielding to others and then berating yourself for your 'door mat' behavior? Decide—to what and whom you need to practice the art of saying 'no'—without feeling guilty for saying it. Be your own person.

5. What are some of your secret yearnings of things you would like to say 'yes' to. Make a list and pick one wish. Give yourself permission to say, 'yes, why not' and do it. It's a great feeling to get out of a rut.

6. Are you a procrastinator? What are the things that you procrastinate about? The incomplete task guarantees you a certain amount of frustration and wasted mental energy. Begin and finish one task and then enjoy the personal good feeling of self-confidence.

Breaking up Relationship Wars

1. Are you a 'naggee'? Do you like waiting for a 'nag'? Do you play a 'blaming game' because the 'nagger' isn't fair? Remember, you are also responsible for keeping the relationship war going.

2. Are you a 'nagger'? Does your nagging pro-

duce the desired results? How do you feel about being a 'nagger'?

3. If there is a relationship war going on, what could you do in a positive way to give to the relationship so the outcome would not be war but peace?

4. Remember, one of the best ways to break up a relationship is to use the element of surprise. For example: If there is a war about keeping a young person's room clean surprise the 'nagger' and do it before the nagging command starts. As a parent you have discovered that you automatically say 'no' to any request from one of your children. Surprise them by thinking about the request and if reasonable, say 'yes'.

5. If you have an 'elephant tape' in that you remember every hurt down to the last detail, make a decision to get rid of it and stay in the present.

6. Little things mean a lot. Have you stopped doing the little things? Be a sensitive lover.

7. Here is a communication exercise for learning a new way to communicate and listen to each other in a marriage. First, the couple should pick a night when they can be alone and the children are asleep. They should take a shower and put on comfortable evening clothes. Both should sit on the floor in the living room with pillows to help them get comfortable and their favorite music playing on the stereo softly. Then one person begins to speak without any interruptions from the other. The first person starts by describing how it feels to sit on the floor, what

muscles he is aware of now and what sounds and odors he senses. He then talks about all of his frustrations in his work and in marriage. This is the time for him to say softly something that he may have held back from the other person, also owning up to his own faults. Then he talks about what he likes about the other person. The silent one is not to start by answering the first speaker but should repeat the same pattern of talking as did the first. After both have spoken, they are to hold each other and enjoy the touching and tenderness.

8. Instead of looking for trouble, look for the good in people. It's so easy for us as a couple or family to become so habituated to respond only to the negatives in other people that the good qualities or acts are easily ignored or passed unnoticed.

Here is an exercise. For one week each person in a relationship agrees to do and say things that are pleasing to the other person or people. Each person is to keep track of every good word or action towards him by another person. Each is also to keep a record of what he said or did to another that was positive. At the end of the week the couple or family discusses their results.

9. Your most valuable possession—your health

(a) When did you last have a good physical?
(b) When did you last see your dentist? Flossing between your teeth and around your gum

line each day will disorganize colonies of bacteria your tooth brush can't reach. Check in with your dentist about your nutrition. Prevention is better than the disease.

(c) Are you overweight?

(d) Do you use alcohol to excess, or sleeping pills or tranquilizers?

(e) Do you exercise regularly?

(f) Do you smoke while being fully aware of the dangers? You can quit, but if you believe you *can't,* you won't.

(g) Are you rushing to die?

(h) Here are some questions asked by Drs. Meyer Friedman and Ray Rosenman in the August 1974 issue of Reader's Digest in the article "Your Personality May be Killing You".

  (1) Do you get upset that you are always falling behind?

  (2) Are you easily irritated when waiting to be seated in a restaurant?

  (3) Are you so competitive that even when you play and lose you become upset?

  (4) Are muscles in your face and hands contracted when you are talking during ordinary conversations?

The type of personality that is prone to more heart attacks is a compulsively driven person, always in a hurry, a high risk taker. He always feels under pressure and finds it very difficult to relax and "hang loose" emotionally. He is explosive and is often known as a "red neck". He is rushing to die without ever discovering why and what he is living for.

10. Write your own philosophy of life. What are your values and priorities in life? What will your obituary say? It is your life, so decide how you want to live and for what purpose.

About the Author

Dr. Kenneth J. Olson received his B.S. degree in psychology from Arizona State College in Tempe, Arizona, and his Master of Divinity degree from Northwestern Theological Seminary in Minneapolis, Minnesota.

For eleven years Dr. Olson served as a Lutheran pastor in California. While there he received professional training in Transactional Analysis with Eric Berne in San Francisco, and Conjoint Family Therapy and Human Communication Theory with Virginia Satir in Palo Alto, California.

In 1965 Dr. Olson returned to Arizona State University to earn his doctorate degree in counseling psychology. He was director of adolescent services at the Mental Health Center in Scottsdale, and founded the Creative Living Foundation in Phoenix for the rehabilitation of drug abusers. He has also served as educational consultant for several Arizona schools and government agencies.

Dr. Olson is currently in private practice as a clinical psychologist in Phoenix. He travels over 100,000 miles a year on speaking tours and has become the most widely known dental psychologist in the United States and Canada.

NON-FICTION

☐	BED/TIME/STORY—Robinson	X2540	1.75
☐	EIGHT IS ENOUGH—Braden	23002-3	1.75
☐	FELTON & FOWLER'S BEST, WORST & MOST UNUSUAL—Felton & Fowler	23020-1	1.95
☐	HOLLYWOOD TRAGEDY—Carr	22889-4	1.95
☐	THE INTRUDERS—Montandon	22963-7	1.95
☐	THE WOMAN SAID YES—West	23128-3	1.95
☐	ANN LANDERS SPEAKS OUT	13946-8	1.75
☐	IT'S ALL IN THE STARS—Zolar	13566-7	1.75
☐	MOON MADNESS—Abel	13697-3	1.75
☐	THE PSYCHIC POWER OF ANIMALS—Schul	13724-4	1.75
☐	THE SECRET POWER OF PYRAMIDS—Schul & Pettit	13986-7	1.95
☐	FROM PLATO TO NIETZCHE—Allen *(Former title Guide Book to Western Thought)	Q768	1.50
☐	THE PSYCHIC POWER OF PYRAMIDS—Schul & Pettit	90001-0	3.95

Buy them at your local bookstores or use this handy coupon for ordering:

FAWCETT BOOKS GROUP
P.O. Box C730, 524 Myrtle Ave., Pratt Station, Brooklyn, N.Y. 11205

Please send me the books I have checked above. Orders for less than 5 books must include 75¢ for the first book and 25¢ for each additional book to cover mailing and handling. I enclose $_____ in check or money order.

Name_____

Address_____

City_____ State/Zip_____

Please allow 4 to 5 weeks for delivery.

BESTSELLERS

☐	BEGGAR ON HORSEBACK–Thorpe	23091-0	1.50
☐	THE TURQUOISE–Seton	23088-0	1.95
☐	STRANGER AT WILDINGS–Brent	23085-6	1.95
	(Pub. in England as Kirkby's Changeling)		
☐	MAKING ENDS MEET–Howar	23084-8	1.95
☐	THE LYNMARA LEGACY–Gaskin	23060-0	1.95
☐	THE TIME OF THE DRAGON–Eden	23059-7	1.95
☐	THE GOLDEN RENDEZVOUS–MacLean	23055-4	1.75
☐	TESTAMENT–Morrell	23033-3	1.95
☐	CAN YOU WAIT TIL FRIDAY?–	23022-8	1.75
	Olson, M.D.		
☐	HARRY'S GAME–Seymour	23019-8	1.95
☐	TRADING UP–Lea	23014-7	1.95
☐	CAPTAINS AND THE KINGS–Caldwell	23069-4	2.25
☐	"I AIN'T WELL–BUT I SURE AM	23007-4	1.75
	BETTER"–Lair		
☐	THE GOLDEN PANTHER–Thorpe	23006-6	1.50
☐	IN THE BEGINNING–Potok	22980-7	1.95
☐	DRUM–Onstott	22920-3	1.95
☐	LORD OF THE FAR ISLAND–Hott	22874-6	1.95
☐	DEVIL WATER–Seton	23633-1	2.25
☐	CSARDAS–Pearson	22885-1	1.95
☐	CIRCUS–MacLean	22875-4	1.95
☐	WINNING THROUGH INTIMIDATION–	23589-0	2.25
	Ringer		
☐	THE POWER OF POSITIVE	23499-1	1.95
	THINKING–Peale		
☐	VOYAGE OF THE DAMNED—	22449-X	1.75
	Thomas & Witts		
☐	THINK AND GROW RICH–Hill	23504-1	1.95
☐	EDEN–Ellis	23543-2	1.95

Buy them at your local bookstores or use this handy coupon for ordering:

FAWCETT BOOKS GROUP
P.O. Box C730, 524 Myrtle Ave., Pratt Station, Brooklyn, N.Y. 11205

Please send me the books I have checked above. Orders for less than 5 books must include 75¢ for the first book and 25¢ for each additional book to cover mailing and handling. I enclose $_____ in check or money order.

Name_____

Address_____

City_____ State/Zip_____

Please allow 4 to 5 weeks for delivery.

FREE
Fawcett Books Listing

There is Romance, Mystery, Suspense, and Adventure waiting for you inside the Fawcett Books Order Form. And it's yours to browse through and use to get all the books you've been wanting... but possibly couldn't find in your bookstore.

This easy-to-use order form is divided into categories and contains over 1500 titles by your favorite authors.

So don't delay—take advantage of this special opportunity to increase your reading pleasure.

Just send us your name and address and 25¢ (to help defray postage and handling costs).